BREAK FREE

How to get free and stay free

Vladimir Savchuk

Unless otherwise noted, all Scripture quotations are from the
New King James Version of the Bible.

DEDICATION

I dedicate this book to everyone who is currently battling with issues bigger than themselves. Help is on the way.

TABLE OF CONTENTS

ACKNOWLEDGMENTS

First, and foremost, I would like to thank my caring, loving, and supportive wife, Lana. Thank you for allowing me to take all the time necessary to finish my work with this book.

This book would not have been possible without the help of Kristina Kovalevich, who did the preliminary editing and the groundwork of polishing my writing. Thank you for leveraging your Hawaiian vacation to help me with this book.

I am especially indebted to Erik Vargas for editing and styling the book. Thank you for carving time out of your summer vacation to help with this project.

Grant Boyer, thank you for giving your expertise to proofread this project. I am thankful to God for your life, it's a blessing to mine.

A huge thanks to Brittany Still for looking at this project with fresh eyes and providing input for the book.

I am grateful to Nazar Parkhotyuk for providing the beautiful graphics for the book cover and promotional material for social media. Thank you for being available to create exceptional graphics for this project.

Thank you, Eder Abogabir, for taking such beautiful pictures of this book and my photo for the author's section. I value your heart and gift to the Hungry Generation family.

A special thanks to Bryson Still for setting up the audio for this book and helping me to mix it.

Nobody has been more important to me in this project than Holy Spirit. He is the One that has taken me from my deliverance to my destiny. He has been with me through thick and thin. This book was birthed out of His prompting. I have sensed His help throughout the working of this project. Thank you, Holy Spirit!

FORWARD

Pastor Vladimir Savchuk is an amazing young pastor whom I've had the privilege of getting to know personally. His dynamic ministry has the courage to focus on matters of spiritual warfare in a bold way.

His book "Break Free" is a much-needed perspective on deliverance and exorcism and covers a wide range of topics that every Christian should be aware of. I especially like his emphasis on the renewed mind in Christ and the importance of keeping the freedom that deliverance brings. Living in Arizona, I found his insight on "dead snakes" personally inciteful.

A helpful Study Guide at the book's end gives the reader an opportunity to quickly grasp the most important points. "Break Free" will help many to escape the bondage of ordinary religion and realize that the destiny of every Christian is to live a life of freedom from unnecessary torment by the Evil One.

Pastor Savchuk is a new, fresh voice calling the church in the Western World to experience an extraordinary life in Christ. I personally expect great things from this book and this unique man of God.

- Dr. Bob Larson

The world's foremost expert on cults, the occult, and supernatural

Author of 37 books, including: "Larson's Book of Spiritual Warfare," "Larson's Book of World Religions," "Demon Proofing Prayers," "Curse Breaking," "Jezebel," "Dealing with Demons" and four fictional novels

REVIEWS

One of the main reasons why Jesus came to this world was to destroy the works of the devil (1 John 3:8). Jesus even stated that he was anointed by the Holy Spirit to set at liberty those who are oppressed (Luke 4:18). Lives being delivered from demonic possession and oppression were among the main manifestations that took place through the life of Jesus. Jesus Himself said, "But if I cast out demons by the Spirit of God, surely the kingdom of God has come upon you," (Mathew 12:28). In the book "Break Free," Pastor Vladimir Savchuk helps us to understand the reality of the spiritual world and how to walk in the freedom that only Jesus can give us. Through his personal experiences, and Scriptural applications you will receive the knowledge and revelation on how to be set free from mental and physical oppression in your own life. As you read this book the works of the enemy will be exposed, and you will discover the decisions that you must make to experience true liberty in Christ. Your eyes will be opened to see how to operate in the power and authority that the Lord has delegated to every one of His disciples. I believe that the Holy Spirit will also use the words in this book to empower you and give you the faith to believe in the abundant life and joy that Jesus promised to those who believe in His name. Get ready to experience the words of Jesus in your own life, "Therefore if the Son makes you free, you shall be free indeed." (John 8:36).

— Andres Bisonni, Evangelist
Author of "My Beloved Holy Spirit"

Pastor Vlad Savchuk's book, "Break Free," is an excellent treatise of the reality of the spirit world and the hold that demonic spirits can have in areas of spiritual bondage. It gives practical steps on how to break free of bad habits and walk in freedom. I highly recommend it for any young person or youth group!

— George Davidiuk, Evangelist

"Break Free" is so captivating to read! It gives the reader solid, simple, and practical directions to walk in liberty. It not only exposes a problem that exists, but gives you detailed guidance to the way out!

— Vadim Pekun, Evangelist

I believe that God raised up Pastor Vlad for such time as this. His sermons are impacting thousands of people around the world. Finally, he published his first book where he shares powerful revelations about the spiritual world and gives practical advice on how to get free and live from the place of victory and freedom. This is the will of God for you — uncompromising, unrelenting freedom. For this, Christ died. For this, He rose. For this, He sent His Spirit. It's time to break free and help others to do the same. Get your copy today. This book will change your life.

— Evelina Smane, Missionary

I believe this book will bring so much hope to people that feel stuck or trapped in bondage. It provides practical steps on how to find freedom in Jesus Christ and points to open doors that the enemy can have in our life. The Bible says, '...know the truth and the truth will set you free.' This book is filled with scripture that will help you renew your mind, especially in this area of life. I strongly encourage you to get a copy, it's worth the read.

— Roman Trachuk, Pastor of Church of Truth

A very deep and important topic is touched in Vlad Savchuk's book "Break Free." I read it, with great interest, in just two evenings. The real-life examples described in this book reveal the truth about the reality of the spiritual world and the authority that God has given to us as believers. Thank you, Vlad, for so openly and sincerely writing about your personal battles and victories. I am sure that, for many, this book will be very relevant and useful.

— Lika Roman, Miss Ukraine 2007
Author of "Amazing Life"

"Break Free" is a powerhouse book! In a culture where the church has strayed away from preaching about demons, strongholds, and deliverance, Vladimir hits these topics head on. And he is DEAD ON! This book is definitely coauthored by the Holy Spirit Himself. I would encourage anyone, whether you are struggling with an issue or you are a minister of the Gospel looking for revelation on how to deal with those who need deliverance... read this book!

— Myles Rutherford, Pastor of Worship with Wonders
Church

"Break Free" is full of powerful revelations that are guaranteed to transform the life of the believer. Vlad clearly explains many Biblical truths that will shift old mindsets and will set believers free to walk in understanding, freedom, and authority. His writing is impactful, memorable, and easy to understand as he uses numerous vivid illustrations, stories, and testimonies. I highly recommend this book not only for personal reading, but especially for small group study along with the study guide. The depth of the many revelations in this book are best absorbed with slow and extended study like a small group setting. I highly recommend Break Free to both new and mature believers.

—Vic Fomenko, Director at California Coast Bible College
Associate Pastor at The City Church – Ventura

"Break Free" is very practical! It gave me tremendous insight to my own struggles as well as others'. It helped me in my personal life and with counseling others. Pastor Vladimir is an amazing speaker and is like an artist in that he paints pictures in your mind as he speaks!

—Rod Brogado, Retired teacher and coach
County Director for Fellowship of Christian Athletes

Honestly, I'm not usually a fan of books that deal in the subject of demonology, because typically these kinds of books focus more on demons than they do on Jesus as the key to deliverance. "Break Free" is the exact opposite. I have never read a book that focuses more on deliverance and walking in the freedom in Christ like this one. I have suggested it to multiple people, because I believe it is an awesome weapon in the hand of every believer, filled with real life stories and nuggets of wisdom on every page!

— Philip Renner, Philip Renner Ministries

Pastor Vladimir has written an excellent book on how to get free and stay free. This book is filled with testimonies of individuals who have experienced deliverance and maintained their freedom. If you have any addictions or habits that you desire freedom from, I highly recommend that you read this book.

— Marlando Jordan, Pastor of Word of Faith

Wherever you are on your walk with Jesus, this is the practical guide to not only gaining true and lasting freedom but recognizing and embracing your true purpose. If you are asking yourself, "Why won't things change in my life?" read this book...they are about to.

— Matt Shea, Washington House of Representatives, 4th Legislative District

"Break Free," by Vladimir Savchuk, is not just a good book title — it's the command and promise of the book. Getting free and staying free is what separates the life message of Jesus Christ from every other religion or philosophy. John 8:36 says, "Therefore if the Son makes you free, you shall be free indeed." All other "freedom" is a counterfeit. "Break Free" will direct you to real and lasting freedom. It challenges you to take all the victory Jesus won on the cross. I am especially impressed with how practical and easy to read this book is. Break free and stay free!

— Mario Murillo, Living Proof Ministries

Spiritual warfare is real, and Pastor Vlad is definitely qualified to write a book on the subject of deliverance. As the pastor of Hungry Generation Church, he has prayed for and witnessed many cases of people being delivered from addictions and demonic oppression. The book is filled with scriptures, stories from personal experience, and testimonies of people. If you want to know the rules of engagement in a spiritual warfare, what tactics to use, and how to pray for deliverance, this book is for you.

— Roman Sheremeta, Ph.D., Professor at Case Western Reserve University

REVIEWS

Pastor Vlad Savchuk has been anointed for such a time as this — to serve this generation. He has been specifically ordained by God and gifted with the ability to lead and show people the way out of slavery and bondage (and not just spiritual, but also mental slavery and bondage). I believe this book is a tool for many to be able to find full freedom and realize their complete potential to live a free life in Christ Jesus.

— Andrey Shapoval, Flame of Fire Ministries
Author of "Predestined"

This is an easy read, a well put together presentation of Pastor Vlad's ministry. His heart comes through each page as it pulls you in from the first page. The topic of spiritual freedom for believers is important since there is no consensus on the demonization of believers. The prayer at the end of each chapter is a great tool allowing readers to search their hearts and apply it personally. The testimonies of Pastor Vlad and the people he has ministered to are powerful. I believe this book will be instrumental to many people in identifying strongholds and obtaining personal freedom.

— Peter Golosinki, Pastor of Connect Church

This book is so timely and needed for this generation. Pastor Vlad shares not only the importance of how to receive freedom in our life, but also how to live free! I love how raw and real Vlad is. His real-life stories and experiences are interesting and powerful. What I loved most in this book is how empowering and possible it is for anyone to walk in freedom. I absolutely recommend this book and will be rereading it over and over! Thank you, Vlad, this is pure gold for our generation!

— Meesh Fomenko, Be Moved Ministries

INTRODUCTION

LION KILLER

It was a usual Thursday night when all the youth would gather for service. Through the entrance walked a tall, handsome, and young man of Italian descent. That night, I gave it my all and I passionately led an altar-call for salvation. This man came running to the front, sobbing and panting before Jesus. As the service ended — people were exiting the sanctuary — the youth gathered around him and listened to him share his story. I overheard him speaking about what he had done and the sins he had committed; telling of his pursuit of sex and money.

He had made a decision to join the religion of Satan. This occurred when he picked up the book of Satan and requested that Satan enter him. I knew I had to lead him in a prayer of repentance, so he could renounce the pact he made with the Devil. He continued to tell the story of why he broke his pact with the Devil. He had a frightening dream of hell, which drove him to throw away all his satanic books. This young man just wanted to live a simple life and no longer desired anything to do with the Devil.

I could not help but interrupt this young man. I asked him if he would repeat a prayer out loud with me so he could renounce any, and all, connection with Satan's kingdom. This simple prayer went as follows, "I repent for making a contract with the Devil. I am sorry for turning my back on God by getting in bed with the Devil. Lord Jesus, deliver me today."

As I said, "Lord Jesus," this man was unable to repeat the prayer. Instead, he began to manifest demonic spirits.

I was only 17-years-old and had only seen demonic deliverances on video, but had never prayed for someone who needed deliverance. At this point, only young people remained and the pastor was already gone. Feeling a mixture of excitement and nervousness, Holy Spirit prompted me to stand further away from him and insist that he pronounce the name of Jesus. An unusual fight took place against the spirit that was tormenting his life. It was a great struggle for him to pronounce the name of Jesus and ask for forgiveness. The color of his face changed and his hand seemed to want to hit somebody. He acted as though someone was holding him back, but no one was touching him. Everyone stood away as he collapsed to the ground.

We were all excited because something miraculous happened. However, there was still one problem. He laid unconscious and I stood in fear! The only thought going through my head was, "This Italian man was killed by Russians at church." Instantly, I remembered the story from the Bible where Jesus cast a demon out of a boy. The boy fell down like he was dead, but the moment he was picked up he came back to life and everything was fine. Our only option was to pick this man up, and after a few minutes he came back to himself.

All of us were curious about what just happened to him. He told us that something came over him. Strong voices insisted that he physically punch us, however, the feeling of someone holding him back overtook him. The young Italian man was shocked to find out that no one was holding him back! Certainly, it must have been God's angels surrounding him during this time of deliverance.

This man's life changed radically after this battle. The following day, when we met, he testified of being healed from a long-term sickness. It was my first time successfully praying for deliverance for someone who was demonized.

Perhaps you have seen videos of deliverance from our ministry. Some manifestations are very physical and loud, while others are quiet with less bodily demonstration. Physical manifestations are not a prerequisite for freedom, however, Holy Spirit's anointing is always a requirement for true deliverance.

Before God publicly used David to kill Goliath, he first had to privately face a lion and a bear. I believe our private victories prepare us for our public triumphs. As I've examined David's life, I suspect he was not too fond of facing a lion. I can imagine these type of thoughts — "Why am I being attacked?" and, "Where is God in all of this?" — must have crossed his mind. When David experienced an attack from a lion and lost a sheep, he could have wallowed in defeat and self-pity. However, David had to make a decision to not live in regret because of his failure of losing a sheep. Thus, he chose to get up and fight to get back what the lion had stolen from him. David did not realize that the battle with the lion would eventually give him the courage and determination to face the giant, Goliath, publicly.

Today, I still believe in deliverance. I believe in deliverance, not just because I have witnessed other people's lives change or because Jesus commanded us to cast out demons, but because I, myself, have experienced freedom from various things that occurred in my life.

At the age of 12, I came across pornographic images. At that time, I did not consider the impact of this exposure, as I did not understand the effects of this material on my life.

I was 13 years of age when my family immigrated to the United States. Everything was new — the country, the friends, and even the language! However, little did I know that I was about to discover a new addiction, which would require God's deliverance.

Six months after our family immigrated to America, my neighbor asked me if I would house-sit for seven days. I was extremely curious to find out how Americans lived. Besides the daily routine of cleaning the house, feeding the cats, and mowing the lawn, I looked forward to checking out the entire house. In doing so, I came across a set of VHS tapes.

The covers of the tapes clearly indicated they had nothing to do with Katherine Kuhlman or the Billy Graham crusades. Be mindful that sin is sneaky and deceptive. The worst part is that you begin to lie to yourself by making up excuses to do what the flesh wants.

After all, I only wanted to double check whether the content in the tapes matched the covers of the VHS. It was evident that it had nothing to do with crusades. It was straight up pornographic material; and instead of turning off the television, I went ahead and watched the entire video. It was at that moment something entered me.

Consequently, guilt and shame overtook me. I felt so disgusted with myself. I immediately promised God that I would never do it again, and quickly repented. Before the week was over I had broken my promise.

In the next few years I found myself engulfed in pornography. Yes, I knew it was wrong, but I could not stop watching it. It did not matter how hard I tried to quit by confessing to my pastor and fasting every week; all it took was one moment of weakness and I was back to sinning.

I knew I could not live like this much longer; I was desperate for freedom! Reality hit when I realized that I was bound to sin and I could not truly be effective in ministry. Also, at that time, marriage was not even an option, as it would mean my future wife would go through much pain while I battled with this issue.

As I began to read books and listen to sermons, Jack Hayford, a well-respected minister, shared a story about one of his deacons who was set free from the spirit of immorality. After many years this deacon approached Pastor Hayford, to confess his struggle with pornography, so Jack Hayford prayed for him.

During that prayer session, Holy Spirit showed Pastor Hayford that there were many holes in his soul. Each hole represented past sexual encounters in his life. Pastor Hayford asked this deacon to go find a specific number of stones, which represented the sum of all his past sexual encounters that resulted in bondages. While he repented and renounced each sexual encounter, the stones were thrown into the east end of the river. After each stone was thrown into the river, he was fully set free.

A dysphoric sensation came over me as I read the book. The Holy Spirit gave me insight that the front door of my soul's house was first exposed to pornography at age 12. Then the back door of my soul's house was opened to the Devil at age 13. Even though these doors were closed, they were not locked!

I spent seven days praying and fasting. Completely broken before Him, I disconnected from everything in my past; including those two vivid encounters in my mind for which I begged for His mercy. Nothing felt different, but I was certain something had changed.

From that point on, a drastic change occurred — something I did not have before was now given to me. I had obtained grace, self-discipline, and the power to control myself when I was tempted.

Today, I walk in freedom and I minister freedom to others. Everyone can experience this type of freedom from God. Nonetheless, freedom is just the beginning and is not the end goal.

You see, the purpose for freedom is so we can fully serve God and fulfill His calling for our lives. Attaining freedom and not fully serving God is equivalent to Israel coming out of Egypt, but failing to enter the promised land. They did nothing to reach their destiny with their newfound freedom.

This book is not just about how to be delivered from demons, addictions, and insecurities. God desires to deliver you from bondage, so He can take you into your destiny.

In this book, I want to show you how freedom is just the first step. The best way to maintain freedom is to use it to grow in God and reach your full potential. This will glorify the name of Jesus in our generation!

Maybe you are like David, facing lions in your shepherd field. Your battles are not meant to kill you, but to prepare you for something greater that will come. God called you to deliver, heal, and save your generation. As you learn how to overcome your private lions, God will shape your character through this process, and impart compassion for those people you are called to reach. Just like with Moses, his escape from Egypt was not just for himself, but to deliver his people from Egyptian bondage! Even Jesus Christ—prior to casting out demons from people—had to face the Devil in the wilderness.

You must win private battles against lions before you win public battles against Goliath. Let us dive in together and learn to identify, confront, battle, and defeat our common enemy.

CHAPTER 1

DON'T BEAT THE DONKEY

Sunday morning, March 9th, a large group of us arrived at a church in Africa. To say God moves powerfully in that ministry would be an understatement. Three times a year we would take different groups from the United States to this church. This time a group of about 50 people was assembled.

While there, a notorious terrorist group by the name of Boko Haram — known for killing over 10,000 Christians in the last decade in Nigeria — was present in our area. Unbeknownst to us, five men strategically mapped out a designated location, near the exit, to detonate a bomb during the Sunday service. Unfortunately, our group also sat very close to that exit door. As you can imagine, everyone sitting near the exit, which included our group of fifty, would have died upon the bomb detonating.

As the service continued, these five terrorists decided to eat at a nearby shop. Since services can last anywhere between 11 to 17 hours on a typical Sunday, time allowed them to indulge themselves before the service came to an end. Meanwhile, the owner of the shop had a live stream of the church service playing on his television. The pastor of the church was prompted to pray for all people, including those watching remotely. The power of Holy Spirit came strongly into that shop. Four of the five terrorists realized they were no match against this type of power, so they quickly ran away from that shop.

One terrorist decided to stay back and fight the presence of God. However, no power can match the power of Holy Spirit. This terrorist ended up falling on the floor and was then dragged into the church by the shop owner. Sitting in the front row, I was not certain who just got dragged in. The pastor came forth and started to pray for his freedom, and the terrorist was completely delivered. His face changed, he began to weep, and he got on his knees to accept Jesus. When he revealed his real intentions of coming to this church, I was flabbergasted.

If it was not for the intervention of Holy Spirit, we would certainly have been dead by the end of that day. What shocked me the most was the radical change I witnessed right before my eyes; from a terrorist to a delivered and saved man. Prior to this, I thought people like him had no chance for redemption because of the overflowing amount of evil within their hearts. On the other hand, God is able to change any person, even a terrorist. God is able to remove all of the evil inside of a man, resulting in the inevitable transformation of that individual.

The First Deliverance Recorded in the Gospels in Jesus' Ministry

There was a time when Jesus went into a Synagogue—under the anointing of Holy Spirit—and an evil spirit within a certain person began to manifest (see Mark 1:21-28). Jesus did not cast the man out of the Synagogue, instead casted the unclean spirit out of the man. However, today, in most churches, if a similar situation of demonic manifestation would occur, the possessed person would more than likely be kicked out or be accused of seeking attention. Jesus was not afraid to do public deliverance. He also did not fear that it would glorify the Devil in any way, or embarrass the person receiving deliverance. When we understand the spiritual world, we know how to attack the demonic forces affecting an individual, while not demoralizing them personally. Because of this, we are able to validate and uphold their true identity in Christ.

If our understanding about the reality of the supernatural realm is distorted or unclear, then we tend to clean up spider webs, instead of first killing the spider. Dealing with the symptoms, instead of the root of the problem, is the dilemma. The spiritual world reveals all the root issues, conversely, the natural world shows the results. The spiritual world created the natural world and contains the source of all issues.

When the Donkey Saw the Spiritual World

It has been my observation that many times unbelievers seem more interested and aware of the spiritual world than the body of Christ. In the book of Numbers, chapter 22, there is a story about a certain man named Balaam who was hired to curse the nation of Israel. God warned him in a dream not to do such a thing. Driven by greed, he decided to disobey God and move forward anyway. He proceeded by riding his donkey to a specific destination. However, the angel of the Lord interfered and stood on the road he traveled upon. The donkey, who was supposed to be blind to the spiritual realm, was given sight to see the angel; whereas Balaam's eyes were sightless to this revelation.

This can be compared to the spiritual state of many believers in our present day. This occurs due to the mentality of fearing what people will say and trying to please others, which causes our eyes to become blind to the reality of the spiritual world. Greed and fear blind us to the invisible realm.

People around us, who are not followers of Jesus Christ, are hungry for the reality of the supernatural and are not afraid of it. Movies, TV shows, songs, and books are filled with the supernatural, plunging people into deeper darkness instead of giving answers to their spiritual pursuits. Just as God used the donkey to wake up and speak to the prophet, I am convinced He is waking up the church, today, to see the hunger the world has for the supernatural. God's authority and influence are superior to any powers of the enemy.

When the donkey saw the angel, "...the donkey turned aside out of the way and went to the field," (Numbers 22:23). Then, "...she pushed herself against the wall and crushed Balaam's foot against the wall," (Numbers 22:25). All this unusual behavior occurred because of opposition to their way in the invisible realm.

When children begin to behave differently by going into addictions and habits that do not glorify Jesus, they turn away from the right path and crush the hearts of their parents. Spiritual forces back up these disobedient actions and we must be willing to combat them.

Balaam was angry, therefore he struck the donkey and almost killed it. He did not realize that the problem was not the donkey but the opposition that originated from the spiritual world that was keeping the donkey from continuing on the path. Let us not make the same mistake as the prophet Balaam.

The Bible is very clear that we are to resist our enemy and do spiritual warfare if we want to walk in spiritual victory. We must deal with the opposition on the road, instead of beating the donkey. The donkey represents the symptoms that may be seen, while the opposing angel on the road speaks of the root of the problem. For example, if there is opposition in our business, we must deal with the root. Also, if there is limitation in our finances, we must deal with the root. Furthermore, if there is stagnation in our spiritual life, we must again deal with the root. Do not just apply more pressure to the donkey — instead open your spiritual eyes and realize that you are in a battle against a real enemy who is after your spiritual progress and breakthrough.

Satan is Behind Sin

Another story bearing witness to the reality of the effects of the spiritual realm is the account of King David numbering the people of Israel. For David, something as simple as numbering the people brought displeasure and judgment from God. "Now Satan stood up against Israel and moved David to number Israel," (1 Chronicles 21:1). David began to trust more in the strength of his military than in the power of God. Pride had opened the door for the Devil, causing David to sin and many people to suffer the consequences of his actions. It is evident that people will get hurt when leaders fail in this magnitude.

What caused David to sin was the following, "...Satan stood up against Israel..." The Devil hates us with every fiber of his being, and he wants to drive leaders into sin. The Devil knows if he can cause leaders to sin, it may crush our faith, or at the least shake our trust in God. It is evident that no one can fall into sin without the assistance of the Devil. Nonetheless, David did not blame his actions on the Devil or others, instead, he admitted his failure and repented. Repentance is the only way we can break the grip of the influence the Devil may have over our choices.

The first sin ever committed by humanity involved the Devil's influence. Adam had no intention to do evil, and no outside culture could sway his decisions. However, a snake in the garden persuaded and deceived Adam to commit an offense. Unlike David, Adam blamed his wife, and subsequently Eve blamed the Devil (the snake). Even though Satan plays his role, it is still our responsibility to repent and allow God to cleanse us. Repentance will never take place if we play the blame game.

When God stepped in, not only were Adam and Eve judged, the snake was also cursed. Adam and Eve were not directly cursed, however, the Devil was; and God was not going to let the Devil off the hook. In fact, He dealt more severely with the Devil than with

11

our first parents, Adam and Eve. Many modern Christians are way too protective of the Devil. For some reason we do not want to deal with the Devil, and instead, we shift all the blame on people. Believers who do deal with demons are labeled as "crazy" or "those people".

There was a time when God had to correct me because I wanted to tone down my stance on spiritual warfare. I knew it was not a popular subject with mainstream Christianity, so I felt I had to water it down. However, Holy Spirit reminded me of the story of King Saul, where he spared the enemy God had commanded him to destroy. When King Saul chose to be too nice to the king of Amalek, Agag, it offended God and He became very displeased. I quickly repented after such a rebuke, and I renewed my decision to not give King Agag any more protection. Satan is God's enemy, therefore, he is also my enemy. I will act as Jesus did, and I will fight as Jesus commanded. Once we resolve this in our heart, God will be pleased and the Devil will be outraged; and, subsequently, many people will be freed.

Deal with the Root, not the Fruit

Jesus showed a unique, but similar, pattern when dealing with people. He is the Creator of the spiritual world. When Christ asked His followers what they thought of Him, Peter quickly responded, "...'You are the Messiah, the Son of the Living God,'" (Matthew 16:16). Jesus did not applaud Peter for such a revelation; instead, Jesus gave credit to the Father, who was the true source of Peter's enlightenment.

Understanding the spiritual world comes from knowing, first and foremost, that all of our advancements and revelations come from God's grace, and not from our merits or good actions. It is impossible to be holy without Holy Spirit. Furthermore, we cannot seek after God until God first pursues us; let us never forget that. Any, and all, glory always belongs to the Lord, for any good that we may do. When we forget this truth, we tend to overlook the valuable lesson Peter learned shortly after his proclamation about Jesus. As Jesus began to share about the sufferings He was about to endure, Peter began to give advice to Jesus. Peter was under the impression that the revelation came from him, therefore, he had a skewed view and proceeded to instruct God.

From a human perspective, Peter was just trying to save Jesus from the sufferings to come. From a spiritual perspective, Jesus discerned that this advice was not from Peter, but from the Devil. The crazy part is that, within the same hour, the great Apostle Peter was first used by Holy Spirit to speak revelation; and then moments after the Devil used him to speak foolishness. We can clearly see that King David — a man after God's own heart, as described in the Bible — and Peter fell prey to pride. Pride is a huge open door for demonic infiltration and even true followers of Christ can fall victim to this. Pride changed a perfect angel into the Devil. This is a great reminder to always give credit to God for any blessings or advances in our life.

The enemy usually has his fingerprints on anything evil in our life. We love to take credit when all is great, yet blame God when things go wrong, and leave Satan untouched. The Devil rarely gets blamed for the evil in the world by the crowds and media.

The architect of all wrongdoing is the Devil. It is evident in Peter's erroneous advice to Jesus, as well as in Peter's denial of Jesus (see Luke 22:31), in Judas' betrayal of Jesus (see Luke 22:3), and when Ananias lied to Holy Spirit (see Acts 5:3). For this reason, the Apostle Paul encourages us to be engaged in spiritual warfare. The fact that we are living on this earth, already makes us involved in this battle; yet not all Christians are engaged in the warfare.

Decisions and Consequences

We know that decisions have either good or bad consequences. However, many bad decisions originate from the influence and effects of the spiritual world. Solomon's son, Rehoboam, made a poor decision of not following the elder's advice to cut back on taxes and reduce the burden on the people. This decision cost him 11 tribes, a devastating loss. Unfortunately, those 11 tribes were never brought back to the house of David. Indeed, bad consequences follow bad decisions. Nonetheless, Rehoboam's bad decision was a result of his father's idolatry. He was unaware that he was set up to fail, because there was a prophecy concerning the 11 tribes and how they would be taken away from King David.

King Rehoboam lacked wisdom for not dealing with the roots of his past, before embarking into his future. Have you ever wondered and asked yourself, "Who is influencing my decisions?" or "Why am I always choosing the wrong people to date?" or "Why do I always seem to make the wrong decisions concerning my finances?" Many Christians will tell you it's because you are not disciplined, not educated, or unwise.

Nevertheless, all these descriptions are outward symptoms, because the real roots lie within the invisible, spiritual realm. Judas' detrimental decision to steal money and betray Jesus was influenced by Satan. All it took was one decision, influenced by dark spiritual forces, to ruin his life. Bad decisions can be the result of demons influencing our lives. For us to make good decisions, we must live under the influence of Holy Spirit.

Spiritual War Removes Evil Out of People

I remember meeting Mel Bond—a powerful minister of the Gospel—through whom God heals and delivers. This took place back in 2013 at Hungry Generation Church. He shared how we could see in the spiritual world. He explained how he saw dark spots or snakes on certain parts of people's bodies when they were afflicted with sicknesses. There were times he would even see a demon. As he would confront that demonic entity, it would leave and that person would receive healing. I, personally, witnessed him do this at our conference. As a matter of fact, God healed Mel Bond, his wife, and children in like manner.

He would first receive a vision and see a dark spirit either sitting on or gripping that part of the body where there was pain. When he commanded it to leave, the healing would come immediately. Jesus said, "No one can enter a strong man's house and plunder his goods, unless he first binds the strong man. And then he will plunder his house," (Mark 3:27).

Natural War vs. Spiritual War

A former president of the Norwegian Academy of Sciences, and Historians from England, Egypt, Germany, and India have tabulated and analyzed some startling data. It is said that in the last 5,600 years, since 3,600 B.C., the world has only known 292 years of peace! During this period there have been 14,351 wars, large and small, in which 3.64 billion people have been killed. The value of the property destroyed would pay for a golden belt that could extend around the world 97.2 miles wide and 33 feet thick. Since 650 B.C. there have been 1,656 arms races, of which only 16 have not ended in war." [1]

A physical war can kill a man, but it is unable to kill the evil within a man. Evil will continue to reside inside a person until a spiritual war removes the evil within. The reason Jesus discourages believers to not be involved in a physical war is because there is a spiritual war that is more significant and impactful. Paul encourages believers to not fight according to the flesh, but to wage war in the spirit. "For though we walk in the flesh, we do not war according to the flesh. For the weapons of our warfare are not carnal but mighty in God for pulling down strongholds…" (2 Corinthians 10:3-4).

Do not Waste the Anointing on Battles Without Spoil

One of the main reasons deliverance did not occur in the Old Testament was that most people were only engaged in physical wars. To be successful at spiritual warfare, we must stop physically fighting other people. "For we do not wrestle against flesh and blood, but against principalities, against powers, against the rulers of the darkness of this age, against spiritual hosts of wickedness in the heavenly places," (Ephesians 6:12). As long as we fight against flesh and blood, we do not possess God's anointing to fight against spiritual forces.

David is a phenomenal example of this. He had to walk away from a battle against his brothers before he fought against Goliath. His brothers provoked him by questioning his motives and heart, which was a way of drawing him into battle. Even though his brothers were soldiers, they were not fighting the real enemy, instead, they battled against their own brother. David chose to walk away from them, to preserve his anointing for the real battle.

We must remember, not every battle is worth fighting. Protect your anointing, so you can fight real spiritual battles. If you are always drawn into arguing, gossiping, defending, and avenging against those who poke you, then you will not have any anointing left to fight the Goliaths in your life. Yes, you may win the battle against your brothers, but you will not have any strength to fight the real enemy, the Devil. For this reason, Jesus remained silent before the Roman Governor, Pilate. His intention was not to battle against the Pharisees and Romans, instead, His only purpose was to fight against spiritual forces of darkness. You may choose to fight and defeat the skunk at any time, but you have to ask yourself, "Is exposing myself to that stench worth the fight?"

Prayer

"Lord Jesus, I come to You as I am, blind to the reality of the spiritual world. As You opened the eyes of Bartimaeus, please open my spiritual eyes. Holy Spirit, anoint my eyes with Your eye salve that I might see. Heavenly Father, let me live in the awareness that those who are with us are more than those who are against us."

CHAPTER 2

SIX DEMONIC SPIRITS

At the age of eight, Kacy was sacrificed to a demon god, Baal, by her father. Her family was part of an occult group. As she grew up demons started to take control of her life. Thoughts about suicide and cutting herself crept in. As time progressed, she was diagnosed with schizophrenia, bipolar, and other mental disorders. Due to excessive mental, emotional, and physical abuse, Kacy lived a lesbian lifestyle for 10 years. This evil spirit caused a lot of mental damage, which needed medical treatment. Because of this, she took 15 different psychiatric medicines, four times a day.

In 2018 she made a decision to attend Hungry Generation's annual "Raised to Deliver" conference. The evil spirit harassing her manifested and was cast out by the power of Holy Spirit. A few months later, she came back to Hungry Generation and shared her testimony of her deliverance. Not only had God set her free from the spirit of Baal and lesbianism, He also had completely healed her. The doctors and professionals advised her that it would take at least two years for her to wean off all 15 of her medications. However, after her deliverance, she stopped taking all those medications; and her body did not experience any negative side effects. She also got connected to a local church and started attending a weekly Bible study; she began to read her Bible daily and memorize Scripture.

This is what it is all about—people being freed to serve God more effectively. No demon can match Holy Spirit, nor possess the power of the name of Jesus. Sometimes, Christians casually throw around words like, "Spirit of that" or "Demon of that," not understanding that life is not a playground, but a battlefield. Satan is no joke, he is a real enemy.

The first mistake most believers make during warfare is underestimating the enemy or lacking the knowledge of who they are coming against. We recognize when watching or observing deliverances, that demons call themselves by their name, such as, "Spirit of Jezebel," "Spirit of rage," and "Spirit of death." There are also times when unclean spirits name themselves after idols, animals, or historic people who were notorious for their evil deeds. Their names reveal their nature and function. Our foundation for spiritual warfare is not built on experiences, but on the Word of God. We see in Scripture that demons can have a name. Jesus shed light on this topic during His earthly ministry.

Legion in the Region

I had the privilege of visiting Israel, and I saw the Sea of Galilee where Jesus calmed the storm, while making His way into a town to deliver a man from a legion of demons (see Mark 4:39).

This particular deliverance revealed that many demons can live in one person, in fact, thousands can reside in an individual. Demons are also behind self-destructive behaviors. A demonized person can exhibit extraordinary physical strength.

In the aforementioned story the possessed man lived in the tombs. Demons prefer hanging out in tombs or cemeteries. Compare this to Holy Spirit Who lives in the believer and makes us temples of the living God. Contrariwise, demons like to make their residence in tombs. You may be wondering why this is the case. Temples are places of life, whereas tombs are places of death. Tombs are places where life used to be. This is why Jesus referred to religious people as tombs — they used to be alive for God, but now they are just a place where demons can visit and dwell. This is why it is extremely dangerous to live on yesterday's manna; living on how God moved, a long time ago, in your life, but currently there is no more passion for Jesus. Yesterday's manna will produce worms, so if you live on what God did yesterday, you will eventually become a tomb where demons prefer to dwell.

Demons can also enter animals, because they are spirits looking for physical bodies. Their main goal is to possess human bodies, but if need be, they will settle for animal bodies. Since pigs were considered unclean by God, it is no surprise that demons entered a herd of pigs. Therefore, unclean spirits will inhabit unclean things.

Out of the Man, but not Out of the Country

There are different spirits that control regions and territories. In the Old Testament, Daniel's answers to his prayers were delayed by the prince of Persia, a strong territorial spirit operating behind the Persian Empire (see Daniel 10:12). The Apostle Paul told Christians in Ephesus that we are fighting principalities, powers, rulers, and spiritual hosts (see Ephesians 6:12). This can explain why some regions of the world have a higher rate of crime, such as murders or violence.

It may shock you to know that Jesus honored the request of demons to let them stay in that region (see Matthew 8:31-32). God also honored Satan's request to attack Job (see Job 1:12). Furthermore, Satan asked to sift Peter as wheat (see Luke 22:31). We do not know exactly why God allowed this, but one thing is certain, it should motivate us to pray and fast more. If Satan, being a rebel, can get his requests honored, then how much more us, who are children of God. When we ask according to God's perfect will, we will receive answers to our prayers.

The demons begged Jesus to stay in that region; conversely the people begged Jesus to leave that region. Jesus honored both of those requests. Yet, the man who was delivered and asked to leave that region and follow Jesus was declined. We can assume Jesus sent him back to the same region which was occupied by those demons. His testimony would have been powerful to help that region. Jesus always leaves His representatives in regions that reject Him, so that through their testimony they can have a second chance to receive Him. When God sets you free, He does it for the purpose of setting others at liberty who are bound by similar spirits.

Demons Speak

What was significant and different about this deliverance is that Jesus interrogated the demon. This shows that demons can speak, however, we are not given any instruction to seek information or have casual conversation with the enemy, but to cast him out. What we do understand is that Jesus did question the demons. There are moments during exorcism that we ask for their name, as Jesus did. We ask, "How did you enter this person?" and "What have you done to this person?" When evil spirits scream, they usually confess that they entered through sin, and they also admit how much they hate prayer. This serves as a reminder to believers that the Devil enters through sin and seeks only to kill, steal, and destroy.

For example, God told Gideon to go to the enemy's camp and listen to what they were saying. God's Word should have been enough for Gideon, but God wanted Gideon to hear the same message from his enemy. We are always telling our youth, "Stay away from sin, honor your parents, and walk close to the Lord," but some refuse to heed these words. However, when they witness deliverances, they see how demons take advantage of people who live in sin, and this brings the fear of God into them. We do not need the Devil to know that prayer is powerful; however, it does bring satisfaction to hear demons scream that prayer is like fire against them. This lets us know that praying and fasting are powerful weapons against the kingdom of darkness.

People who come and receive prayer at our church or conferences are required to sign a media release form, which gives us permission to share their testimony online to glorify God. There have been times that pastors have criticized this practice. They claim that sharing this content with the public embarrasses people and elevates the Devil. On the contrary, we have found that this proves deliverance embarrasses the Devil, builds people's faith, and instills God's fear in this new generation. Jesus refused to exclude deliverances from any of the Gospels, nor did He perform them in private. He did not do them for show, but to glorify God and bring help to those struggling.

Names of Demons Reveal the Nature of Demons

The Scriptures reveal the names of demons, as an indication to the nature of their activity in the lives of people. We know that demons are fallen angels who serve Satan (see Revelation 12:8-9). Demons are called evil spirits, unclean spirits, familiar spirits, lying spirits, and angels of Satan. Since the Devil is not God, he cannot be in all places at once, so he does most of his dirty work through his demonic agents.

Their goal is to entice, harass, torment, enslave, cause addictions, defile, deceive, and attack the physical body. Let us look at some of the names of the evil spirits, that are mentioned in Scripture.

Spirit of Fear

The Bible says that there is a spirit of fear (see 2 Timothy 1:7). The Apostle Paul writes to Timothy, the young pastor, to tell him that God has not given us a spirit of fear. This type of fear is different from natural fear, which is given to us by God to protect us from natural harm. This also differs from the fear of the Lord, which is to be in awe of God and bestow honor on Him. A spirit of fear is extremely demonic, because it paralyzes our potential and it imprisons us. As a matter of fact, everything in the kingdom of Satan is run by fear. On the other hand, everything in God's kingdom operates by faith. We must understand that demons cause unnatural fear to invade our lives; such as fear of circumstances, death, driving a car, or of other people. For these reasons, people can experience fear of going insane, chronic timidity, paranoia, fear of isolation, fear of failure, fear of losing their job, fear of getting married, fear of getting sick, trepidations, and nightmares.

After marrying my beautiful wife, she began to be attacked by an evil spirit during the night when she slept. She was constantly having scary nightmares. There were times I woke up from her crying due to pain she experienced in her sleep. These nightmares really affected her mood during the day, causing our relationship to suffer. They created feelings of loneliness, making it very difficult for her to work and be in ministry. Many of us are enticed to think that these are just emotions, and I thought in this same manner. In time, we found that this had a deeper root than just her emotions. This situation was affecting us greatly, because it was occurring every other night. We came to the understanding that this issue was demonic. We, then, stood against this opposition and also involved others to pray for our situation. After this, the evil spirit was defeated, and power, love, and a sound mind became part of my wife's new lifestyle. Fear will always want to control us, limit our potential, and cripple our inner joy. God never gives us a spirit of fear, instead, He is a very good Father and gives us the spirit of love and goodness.

Spirit of Lust

The spirit of lust, or immorality, is the most prevalent spirit in our culture (see Hosea 5:4). This spirit of lust is the evil force behind pornography, adultery, fornication, prostitution and homosexuality. Many times, this demon will bring sexual dreams, and will make it appear as our spiritual husband or spiritual wife. This demon drives singles into premarital sex and conversely, this same spirit, pulls married couples apart, and keeps them from enjoying true intimacy in marriage.

The spirit of lust is not really interested in sex, but its sole purpose is for us to fall into sin. The fruit of this lust will never last and it is never satisfied. Most people who are involved in these lustful behaviors will indicate that it was not just the flesh they were satisfying, but that something else was driving them to commit these acts.

I, myself, was delivered from the spirit of pornography, and I can testify that at certain times this evil spirit would overtake me and would drive me over the edge. I do not blame the Devil for my actions. However, I came to the realization that no matter how hard I tried to stop, repent, and promised to never do it again, I would once again fall back into indulging in pornographic materials. I truly hated the predicament I was in.

Spirit of Bondage

Many people do not realize that behind all addictions is a spirit of bondage (see Romans 8:15). This demon drives people to become addicted to alcohol, drugs, smoking, gambling, and video games.

There are also lighter addictions that are attributed to this spirit, such as being addicted to food, television, cell phone, computer, money, work, sleep, and persistent tardiness. Many recovery programs are not effective, because they fail to deal with the spiritual root of the addiction. Addiction can be compared to a spider web, and the demon to a spider. Until we kill the spider, cleaning the spider webs will be completely ineffective.

A leader at a certain church once shared a testimony about his freedom from smoking. After becoming a Christian, he was unable to quit smoking. Then, after a particular evening service, he took a walk on a certain street, and God suddenly opened his eyes to the spiritual world. He saw two demons sitting on electrical wires, and he heard their conversation. One demon said to the other, "Look he is coming from church, he is going to quit smoking." The other demon replied, "He will smoke after I do this." This demon pulled a string and, immediately, this church leader began to have an urge to smoke. At that moment he realized that his urge to smoke resulted from this demon pulling a string. A holy anger then came over him, and he resisted the Devil's influenced urge to smoke. From that moment on, he was set free, never to smoke again. As Holy Spirit gives us His desires, conversely, the Devil will also try to implant strong urges to drink, smoke, watch porn, gamble, cheat, and do other immoral things.

Spirit of Infirmity

Another spirit that we find in Scripture is the spirit of infirmity (see Luke 13:11; Mark 9:25). Often, these demons are behind allergies, diabetes, arthritis, cancer, constant weakness, mental disorders, back problems, organ failures, nerve disorders, chronic rashes, and fungal infections. This should not surprise us because Jesus healed those who were oppressed by the Devil (see Acts 10:38). God did not give sicknesses to people; it is evident that people are under demonic oppression when their physical bodies are sick.

If sickness was from God, then any attempt to go to the doctor and take medicine would be a direct insult to the will of God. Sickness is always from the evil one. We acknowledge this fact Monday through Saturday, but on Sunday, for some reason, we act as if it is a good thing to be sick. Jesus took all of our infirmities to the cross with Him, along with all of our sins. Everyone who came to Jesus during His earthly ministry and asked for healing, was healed. His finished work on the cross is our standard. You may ask, "What about Job?", "What about Paul's thorn?" Jesus is our standard, not Job or even Paul. Jesus is God. He is the best revelation of the nature of the Father. I don't see any instances where someone who was sick, and asked Jesus to heal them, was refused by Him.

It is interesting to note that Jesus did not pray for healing, He simply healed people. He rebuked sicknesses, even an ordinary head fever (see Luke 4:39). Jesus also commanded a certain woman to be free from back issues that had troubled her for eighteen years (see Luke 13:12). The Gospel of Luke makes it very clear that Jesus did not say, "Be healed from your sickness," because her illness was a result of demonic oppression. Jesus confirmed this fact by saying that Satan had bound her for eighteen years (see Luke 13:16).

One reason we do not see more healings is because we only pray for healing, instead of casting out the spirit of infirmity. During one of our conferences, a man traveled from another state to receive healing. He had a severe case of leukemia. However, due to his late arrival, he missed the prayer line. Still, during the service, there was corporate prayer for those in the audience. Holy Spirit fire came down into our sanctuary, and unclean spirits begin to manifest and be removed. This man found himself on the floor throwing up, being delivered in Jesus' name. When he went back home, he had blood work done and doctors confirmed that he was completely healed. He repeated this blood work every six months, and each test has confirmed that he has remained healed, for the glory of God. The moment the spirit of sickness is cast out, healing follows.

Another time, one of the young couples on our team brought their mother for prayer. This woman had chronic sleep apnea, so she slept with a machine during the night, and was always tired. During our prayer line, this evil spirit of sleep apnea was cast out. She felt perfectly fine when she went home and was able to take a nap without her breathing machine. After this, when a doctor examined her he confirmed that she was totally free of any sleep disorder. The spirit of infirmity can bring terminal sickness, but the Spirit of God will always bring permanent solution to that sickness.

We see in the Scriptures and from our experience that demons can bring sickness. However, this does not mean that every person who is sick is demon possessed. The Bible does not teach or give credence to this idea.

Spirit of Pride

The spirit of pride is also a real demon (see Proverbs 16:18). As Solomon teaches us, this spirit goes before destruction. This means that before the Devil can bring destruction, he first sends a demon by the name of pride. This spirit brings arrogance, revenge, rebellion, egotism, lust for power, criticism, anger, independence, cruelty, and jealousy.

In essence, pride is the idolatrous worship of self. Pride is the national religion of hell. In fact, the amount of pride a person has is equal to the amount of demons within. Pride transformed Lucifer, the anointed cherub, into Satan (see Ezekiel 28:14). This evil spirit will definitely destroy everything it enters.

Pride will create an open door in our hearts for the Devil to bring defeat. In other words, self-righteousness brings pride, and pride attracts demons, and this demon brings defeat. When Jesus told His disciples that every one of them would eventually forsake Him, Peter disagreed. Peter was overconfident and proud of his commitment to Jesus. The Devil then took advantage of this, and for this reason, he asked to sift Peter and not the other disciples (see Luke 22:31).

When we yield to the spirit of pride, it will eventually bring us destruction. Thus, it is best to walk in humility, for this posture will attract Holy Spirit and His power.

Spirit of Python

Lastly, there is a demon called the spirit of python or spirit of divination (see Acts 16:16). This spirit operates through the occult like Free Masonry, Scientology, secret societies, New Age, eastern religions, fortune telling, chain letters, black and white magic, calling forth the Devil, hypnosis, numerology, Satanic worship, water witching, levitation, charms, Ouija boards, horoscopes, zodiac signs, and dream catchers.

I have a good friend, who is a great pastor, whose daughter recently received deliverance from the spirit of python. This spirit came into her through smoking weed, dabbling in the occult, and specifically from Free Masonry. Yet, no snake is a match for the Lamb of God, therefore, she was freed from this tormenting spirit.

Python always seeks to deceive. There was a certain girl in the book of Acts, chapter 16, who was possessed and was prophesying correctly under this demonic influence. If the Apostle Paul did not have the gift of discernment, he would have requested that this girl assist him in spreading the "Good News."

The first Biblical account of the Devil was when he entered our world as a snake. Also, the last mention of the Devil was in the form of a snake.

Python is different from most snakes. It is interesting to note that most insects bite to suck blood, snakes bite to release poison, but the python kills by squeezing its victim. This spirit of python is after our spiritual breath. It will choke to death our spiritual life with Holy Spirit, and it accomplishes this by manipulation, intimidation and domination.

Unlike Holy Spirit, demons always seek to control, dominate, and intimidate people. We must be cautious not to fall prey to this spell. Anyone who speaks in God's name, but attempts to control and dominate people is still under the influence of this unclean spirit. Contrariwise, Holy Spirit is like a dove; He does not force, control, deceive, manipulate, or intimidate. Thus, it is vital that those in leadership guard their heart against the spirit of python.

As we can see, demons have names, and their names reveal their actual function. It's possible that some of these spirits mentioned above, may be active in your life today. Nevertheless, be assured that there is true freedom for you in Jesus. This wonderful freedom is as real as the bondage you may be currently in.

Prayer

"Dear Jesus, thank You for sending Your Holy Spirit into my heart. Give me the strength to resemble the nature of the dove. I repent for any sin of manipulation. Forgive me, if I have used my position to dominate and intimidate others. I repent for any pride and overconfidence that has made me act more like the Devil. I repent of any spirit of lust that I have allowed to run rampant in my life. Forgive me, Father!

BREAK FREE

I expel every spirit of fear and receive the spirit of power, love and a sound mind. I expel every spirit that is behind any bondage or addiction. Any demonic activity behind my sickness and pain, I command it to be gone in Jesus' name. I stand against every form of intimidation, domination, and manipulation used against me. Holy Spirit, thank You for Your help."

CHAPTER 3

OPEN DOORS

One of my biggest pet peeves is having open doors. I won't pray until all the doors in the room or sanctuary are closed. I am constantly aware of open doors. My wife and I have always had people living in our home. So, I remind those living in my house to close all the doors and windows before they leave the house. There was a time when we had an event at a local park, where our worship team was playing. We were at the park all day, so it was dark by the time we got home.

When I entered our house and stepped into our living room, I suddenly felt a breeze of wind. At that moment, I thought I was experiencing something spiritual like in the book of Acts, chapter 2. Afterwards, I heard a noise coming from the street through one of the rooms. As I began to make my way to that room, I noticed that many drawers were pulled out in the kitchen, and I also saw stuff hanging from the shelves. The moment I entered the room, I saw the entire room was in disarray, as though a devastating tornado had gone through it. Everything in this room was turned upside down. Furthermore, I noticed that the window screen protector was removed and left next to the window. There were glove prints all over the drywall and on the window frame of the window that had been left opened.

We came to the realization that an intruder had entered our home while we were at the park. It was indeed a scary feeling, and we had an awful sense of invasion, because this intruder had infringed on our privacy. This intruder had gone through all of our stuff, including things in the garage. Oddly enough though, I noticed that the computer, iPad, jewelry, and everything else was still in its original place. None of our belongings were missing, except for the vehicle. Ironically, the vehicle that was stolen did not even belong to us. This car was loaned to us, because we had given both of our vehicles away. Our home had been broken into, but only that vehicle was missing.

It is evident that this thief had studied us, and waited for the opportune time — when everyone had left the house — to break in. He was successful because all it took was for one person to leave the windows unlocked.

After we had filed the police report, something very interesting transpired. The person who stayed in this particular room — the room by which the thief entered our home — was the same person who saw our stolen car in a nearby parking lot, while dropping off some people. When the police arrived, they found a note in the car that read, "I am sorry for stealing your car." Fortunately for us, the thief had a change of heart. We also learned a very valuable lesson that day! If we want to protect ourselves from a thief, we must ensure that our doors and windows remain locked, for a thief is always looking for an open door.

Satan is a thief; and, like a thief, he operates best at night (see John 10:10). He loves to work secretly and anonymously. After his satanic activity, something always goes missing in our life. However, there is a difference between losing something and having it stolen. We lose things by negligence, but many times we are able to find these items when we remember where we left them. On the other hand, when something is stolen, it is always the work of a thief.

When joy, peace, or purity go missing, you can be sure that the Devil – like thief, has gone through your life and stolen from it. But like a thief, he can't steal if we have our life secured in holy living. Satan is always studying us to find an open window of opportunity which he can use to come in and take things. You have to understand, the thief never moved into my house to live there, but he visited it and took something. If Satan can't possess you by living in you, he will try to harass you by taking things from you if you leave an open window of compromise.

Sin is the Trojan Horse

Satan can only work when sin is committed. God cannot work without our faith and, in like manner, Satan can do nothing without the existence of sin. Sin is his access to a person's life. Scripture warns, "...nor give place to the devil," (Ephesians 4:27). This Scripture is written to admonish Christians. As Christians, we can open our lives to the Devil when we give in to sinful behaviors. Adam and Eve came under the dominion of Satan through their willful act of sin. However, "the prince of this world" had nothing on Jesus, because of His sinless life (see John 14:30).

There is a well-known story about the Trojan War, where the Greeks used a wooden Trojan horse to enter the enemy's city and win the war. After a fruitless 10-year siege, the Greeks made a huge wooden horse and hid a few powerful men inside. The people inside that city thought it was a gift from the Greeks and did not realize that it was only a trap. Likewise, sin always seems like a gift, fun and games, but it is a trap from the devil.

In Genesis, chapter 3, we are given insight as to the characteristics of the Devil. He is cunning, sneaky, and deceptive. Sin is not only an offense to God, it is direct rebellion to His will. Sin is also an open door by which the devil can attack, oppress, and, in some cases, possess an individual.

Our enemy always presents sin as something desirable that we should fall in love with. However, behind the scenes, sin always has a hidden agenda that is set in motion by the prince of darkness.

This tactic is revealed in the story of Delilah and Samson (see Judges 16). Samson fell in love with Delilah, a Philistine woman, but this was a forbidden romantic relationship. Samson's enemy, the Philistines, took advantage of this love affair and conspired with Delilah to defeat Samson. Delilah only pretended to love Samson, but the entire time she was reporting back to the Philistines her progress in discovering Samson's secret to his supernatural strength. In fact, she had Philistines in her house ready to apprehend Samson the moment he lost his extraordinary strength. The Philistines paid Delilah to collaborate with them.

Likewise, sin is like Delilah, it gives momentary pleasure, but sin's only allegiance is to do Satan's bidding. Sin does not care about our wellbeing. While we are having fun with sin, Satan has already prepared demons to attack, torment, and oppress us. As the Philistines were behind Delilah's actions to bring Samson down, in like manner, Satan uses this tactic to accomplish his mission of defeating you. For Samson, Delilah was the open door, which the Philistines used to defeat him. Now, let us look at some open doors that the Devil uses, in our generation, to enter and defeat us.

The Door of the Occult

The word "occult" literally means "hidden from view."[2] It is something hidden, secret, and mysterious. The occult is astrology, witchcraft, the black arts, fortune telling, black magic, white magic, Ouija boards, spiritism, tarot cards, horoscopes, and talking to the dead. All these practices are huge open doors for demons to enter our lives. The occult also includes partaking in false religions that directly or indirectly worship the Devil. Christians should never get involved or fall into these demonic practices.

There was a time, that I will never forget, when we were praying for a certain young man who was possessed by many demons. These demons entered him when he went to a grave yard and invited the Devil in. This young man was angry with God, because his brother had recently died. Right there at the grave yard, something entered him. He changed after that. Violence, anger, and rebellion entered him. He was expelled from school and later put in jail for his behavior. Throughout all of this, he still considered himself a Christian. During our Sunday morning service, the demons operating in his life couldn't stand to be in the presence of God, so they manifested. He was delivered, repented from his sin, and God restored him.

It is my conviction that genuine Christians should never do this, because when we step into the Devil's territory, demons will come and attack us. There are also times that parents dedicate their own children to demons, and this results in demons entering them. I still recall one of the most violent deliverances I have ever witnessed. This deliverance involved a young girl who was dedicated to Satan by her parents, who became witches through a blood covenant. This girl was 17 years of age when she visited our Sunday morning service with her friends from another state. During prayer, demons manifested and, by the power of Jesus, they were cast out. I was reminded that day that there is power in dedicating babies — it either works for good or evil, and the spiritual world is fully aware of this.

In the Old Testament, God removed pagan nations by giving the nation of Israel power to drive them out, because of their divination, sorcery, and witchcraft (see Deuteronomy 18:9-14). God also warned His people, Israel, that they should not get involved in these demonic practices, or else He would turn His face against them (see Leviticus 20:6). From the Scriptures, we learn that the nation of Israel fell into worshipping idols, witchcraft, and necromancy — all practices that offended God.

As Christians, all of us get tempted; and we can fall into sin because of our fleshly desires. But deliberately going to the kingdom of Satan for help, or out of curiosity, will be detrimental to your soul. There are people who consult witchdoctors for healing and breakthrough. On one hand, Satan can give you a healing or a breakthrough, and on the other hand, he will take away your freedom. Thus, you will be caught by his dark kingdom, whose only purpose is to destroy. Nevertheless, most people in our generation seek the kingdom of darkness out of curiosity, thinking it is an innocent act. However, there is nothing innocent about it.

As a child in Ukraine, I had an experience where a dog bit me and I had to get stitches. The owner of the dog was my neighbor and was also my math tutor. I would go to her house and she would help me with my math deficiencies. As long as her dog was on a leash, he was unable to hurt me; the only thing he could do was bark, and not bite.

The spiritual world is similar. As long as we are in the kingdom of God, Satan can only tempt, but not torment us. Yet, there was a time when I went to her house for tutoring and I noticed that the dog was not at his usual location. I assumed he was somewhere else, but my curiosity got the best of me. So, I decided to stick my head into the dog house, and to my surprise the dog was laying behind his house. The dog then jumped on me and bit pieces of skin off of my leg. Fortunately, the owner of the dog also happened to be a doctor, and came to my rescue and stitched me up.

If you get involved with the occult, you are stepping onto the Devil's territory. You can be sure he will bite—he will attack and bring torment into your life. Whatever reason you have for doing this foolishness, you must repent today from this sin, renounce it, and forsake it. If you are already being tormented because of your involvement with the occult – Jesus is your only hope for deliverance.

The Door of Accursed Things

We need to understand that power flows through people, places, animals, and objects. In the Bible, demons were able to possess pigs (see Matthew 8:28-34). God can use any medium by which He can express Himself. He can also use physical objects, like Moses' rod, to manifest His power to perform miracles (see Exodus 4:3). God also used the Jordan River to heal Naaman (see 2 Kings 5). He can also use oil for healing (see James 5:14). In another account Jesus used His saliva to bring healing to a blind man (see Matthew 8:22-26). Furthermore, the very clothing that Jesus wore, God used to stop chronic bleeding that a certain woman suffered from (see Matthew 9:20-22). Moreover, handkerchiefs and aprons that were touched by the Apostle Paul brought deliverance to the oppressed (see Acts 19:12). Conversely, the Devil is a copycat; and he cannot create, but only duplicate. This is why most sorceries operate through objects, such as charms and dream catchers.

There is a story in the Old Testament, where a man named Achan took what was forbidden while fighting in the battle of Jericho. He not only transgressed God's covenant, but also brought a curse on the entire Israelite camp, which resulted in the death of 36 soldiers, in addition to the execution of his entire immediate family (see Joshua 7:11-25).

There are certain objects that are dedicated to demons that must be destroyed, and these items must not be allowed into our homes. Witches and wizards pray for charms to do their dirty work. Many of these charms are given and sold in shops, and they can bring many curses into people's lives. The Bible declares, "Nor shall you bring an abomination into your house, lest you be doomed to destruction like it. You shall utterly detest it and utterly abhor it, for it is an accursed thing," (Deuteronomy 7:25). This is why during a revival in Ephesus, people were burning their occult books (see Acts 19:19).

During our church conference, a certain church member brought her sister for prayer. Her sister was unable to work due to uncontrollable crying. Our prayer team prayed for her, which resulted in her throwing up profusely, and she felt relieved afterwards. However, that very next day, on Monday — when she stepped into her house — the whole crying situation began again. After receiving a phone call, we arrived at her home, I noticed she was on her knees in the bathroom floor throwing up and crying uncontrollably. She was unable to talk. We began to walk back and forth, praying in the house, as she remained in the restroom. I asked God to show me the cause of this madness in her life.

Then I saw a little paper hanging over the inside of the door entrance, which had Spanish words written on it. It contained the word "diablo," which means "Devil" in Spanish. I asked her why it hung there, and she replied that some lady in Mexico gave her ex-boyfriend this prayer note to guard their house. Initially, it seemed innocent, but for some reason I had a weird feeling about it. She went on to say that her ex-boyfriend, while visiting Mexico, went to this old lady — who mixes the occult with religion — who then pronounced "blessings" over him. This old lady gave him some items in addition to this prayer. This witch guaranteed that if their relationship failed, bad things would happen. So, the moment her boyfriend broke up with her she began to throw up and cry tremendously.

We decided to remove the items given by the witch, along with the written prayer, and dispose of them in the garbage. The moment those items left her hands, her face immediately changed, and the crying and vomiting instantly stopped. Thereafter, her life returned to normality, and she went back to work as a nurse. Eventually, her boyfriend also came to our prayer line for salvation and deliverance. This is an example of how objects, prayers, and charms—given by servants of Satan—have the power to bring demonic spirits.

Houses can also be cursed—the world calls them "haunted houses" for a reason. Often if a murder or suicide occurs at a certain place, then evil spirits can begin to mark that territory, and malevolent things can develop and affect those who move in. It is crucial to always say a prayer of dedication, to cancel any assignment the enemy may have over that home.

There is a local story in our town, where a certain person committed suicide in a house. Afterwards, the house was rented out, and all three couples that moved in eventually got divorced. Furthermore, there was another time where a different person, who also moved in heard noises and witnessed furniture move at night. This paranormal activity is real, so we should not be surprised if the Spirit of God is also real. There are certain places where God's Spirit is more tangible, because of people's prayer and fasting. This is why people can walk into physical structures—like churches and auditoriums—and feel God's love, peace, and joy.

This same principle applies to vehicles. There is a story of James Dean, a car racer, who owned a Porsche Spyder that was referred to as the "Death Car" or "Little Bastard". James Dean acquired this vehicle to race in Salinas, California. Many of his friends did research on this car, and warned him not to drive it or else he would be dead within a week. This is exactly what happened. A week later, James Dean died on the way to the race track in a terrible car accident.

Because this race car had been driven by a very famous person, all the parts of this vehicle were sold for a high price. The engine from Dean's original car was placed into another car, which was later involved in an accident that killed the driver. Then another driver bought the drivetrain that was part of the "Little Bastard," and also got injured when his vehicle rolled over. It was also reported that two of the tires went to a young man. These two tires happened to blowout at the same time while in a race, causing him to lose control and end up in a ditch. Additionally, while the Porsche Spyder was being stored in a Californian garage; that structure caught on fire and everything was destroyed, except for the car. Later on, a truck driver was transporting this car and lost control of his truck, and apparently the "Little Bastard" fell off the flat bed and crushed him to death. There were even more examples that happened than what I have mentioned here, but this is a good reminder for you to pray for your vehicle as well. You never know what has happened to it and who drove it for what reasons. You want that vehicle to lead you from point A to point B, not to your funeral or to have a terrible accident.[3]

It is possible that we may have bought, inherited, or received a gift such as voodoo dolls, snakes, dragons, Pokémon, art of pagan worship items, books for Satanic horoscopes, porn magazines, good luck charms, or dream catchers. We must be willing to throw these items away and renounce any connection that Satan may have over our home or life.

Also, if we were in any kind of romantic relationship that ended, it is prudent to dispose of all the gifts and items given to us by that person. These items can hold emotional soul ties that can affect a future relationship.

I am persuaded, and it is my conviction, that followers of Jesus have no business celebrating Halloween. The founder of the Church of Satan said, "I am glad that Christian parents let their children worship the Devil at least one night out of the year." What the birth and resurrection of Jesus means to us, in like manner, Halloween has the same significance to the world of the occult.

Halloween promotes fear, darkness, and death; Christianity promotes love, light, and life.

Avoid getting on the Devil's territory by bringing demonic objects into your house. Every residence you move into or car you buy, pray a special prayer of dedication for it. And don't participate in the fruitless works of darkness by taking part in events that clearly honor the Devil.

The Door of Trauma

When I had dinner with Bob Larson — who has performed over 30,000 deliverances and is widely considered the world's expert on the occult and exorcism — I asked him, "What is the common door that most demons enter in throughout our western countries?" He informed me that in all other continents most demonic cases are due to the occult, while in western countries it is usually due to abuse.

Therefore, demons can enter through abuse, trauma, rejection, sexual abuse, rape, and molestation which create inner hurts and unforgiveness in people. It seems unfair that, at no fault of their own, people experience these terrible events. It is bad enough they were victimized, and now they have to deal with the spiritual repercussions. When my house got broken into, it was not me who left the window open to the thief, it was someone who lived in my house. We must understand that decisions of others, such as our family members, can open our lives to spiritual attack.

There are incidents where the spirit of rejection enters people, because their parents never wanted them. This is the case for many children who were born as a result of a "one-night stand" or premarital sex. I grew up in a strong, traditional Pentecostal culture, where you are expected to have as many kids as possible. Family planning, or using other preventive methods to avoid having kids, was unacceptable. Many kids who were born into big families experience this rejection from their mothers, since the family was already too large. This may seem trivial, but this can create a spirit of rejection in the life of that child. That rejection will manifest later on in life, through rebellion or other bad behaviors.

I have met countless mothers, who did not want to have many kids, but church dogma forced them. They gave birth to children who were a burden to them, and these children grew up, and acted differently than other children. When these children grew up, Holy Spirit revealed to them that the cause of feeling rejected was planted in them — through the spoken words and attitudes of their parents — while they were still in their mother's womb. Many of these children were troubled throughout their lives.

These mothers must come to God and their children in repentance. They need to pray with them to remove any trace of rejection, because this can lead to rebellion. If you were an unwanted child — and you observe the spirit of rejection and rebellion in your life — then you can also be free in Jesus' name.

Rejection in the womb is not the only way trauma and rejection occur. Growing up without a father is another big way. We live in a fatherless generation. The majority of murderers grew up without dads. Most school dropouts have no fathers. Homeless and runaway kids are often from fatherless homes. The abuse of children has increased drastically in recent decades. Sexual abuse has skyrocketed. The absence of the father is as damaging as the rejection in the womb. That rejection breeds rebellion. We punish rebellion, but rarely deal with the root of this which is rejection.

"Repent therefore of this your wickedness, and pray to God if perhaps the thought of your heart may be forgiven you. For I see that you are poisoned by bitterness and bound by iniquity," (Acts 8:22-23). Simon, the witchdoctor who used spiritual powers as a means to control people, was bound by iniquity. The Apostle Peter, through Holy Spirit, revealed the real issue. Simon, the witchdoctor, was poisoned by bitterness which led to his severe bondage. Simon was already saved and baptized, but these roots of bitterness were left untreated. The poison of bitterness opened the door for the bondage of iniquity. If you think you have a right to be bitter, then Satan thinks he has a right to keep you bound. If you want to be free from this demonic grip, you must uproot the poisonous root of bitterness with the shovel of forgiveness.

Many of us are familiar with the parable that Jesus shared about how a certain servant was forgiven a huge debt, but he, in turn, refused to forgive his servant who owed him a little (see Matthew 18:34). Thus, the master delivered him to the torturers. The torturers are the demons who enter and oppress through the open doors of offense and bitterness. When we receive forgiveness from God and then refuse to give forgiveness to those who hurt us, it opens the door to demonic torment.

There was a young lady who was living a lesbian lifestyle, and got invited to one of our conferences through social media. She indicated that as a little girl she was molested by a family relative. She explained that she felt something enter her after that incident. During our prayer, an evil spirit manifested, and by the power of Holy Spirit, the demon was removed. Today – through the renewing of her mind and discipleship – this young lady is on our team serving and growing in Christ. The spirit of lesbianism has become a part of her past.

I am convinced that it is not just the abusive act that automatically sends demon, but our response to that experience. Many heroes in the Bible, including our Savior, went through huge rejections, yet remained committed to God.

Betrayal is what happens to us, bitterness is our response to it. Betrayal is what people do, and bitterness is what we allow to grow. Instead we must learn to confess our sin, forgive those who hurt us, confront the enemy, and become part of a community of believers. We must also receive counseling and, in time, those wounds will heal.

Every open door can be closed through our repentance. In turn, repentance will lead us to a life of holiness and freedom.

Prayer

"Father God, Your Word says that Jesus is the Door for the sheep. Through ignorance and foolishness, I have opened the doors to the occult in my life. I deeply regret this and I repent of it. I choose to remove any ungodly objects from my house and car. Jesus, cleanse my life by Your blood. Oh, Holy Spirit, cleanse my life from any trace of rejection by the fire of Your love. I receive Your Word today, that I am accepted in You, and I close any open doors right now. Jesus, I open the door of my heart to You and Your Word."

CHAPTER 4

GRAVE CLOTHES

The first time I met Eder was on the soccer field. We both share a love for soccer. After playing a game with us, I invited him to our home group. Although neither of us could speak English very well, I used whatever English I knew to bring him to a closer relationship with Jesus. Though this young man had given his life to Jesus, he still partied on weekends. After some time, he moved to New York — where he met the love of his life, Tatiana — and shortly after got married. Both Eder and Tatiana came from broken families, where marriages ended in divorce. I warned him, while he still resided in the Tri-Cities, about the generational curse of divorce. I advised him that he would have to face this generational curse one day. I also informed him that his "weekend partying" was giving leeway to the Devil, and would cause him to repeat the destiny of his parents.

Shortly after his marriage, I received a message from his wife that Eder was confused and that he was planning to leave her. There were no arguments or affairs of any kind. In fact, everything was going well. This all happened suddenly, and then feelings of being trapped overtook him and his beautiful dream. What seemed odd to me was that she was everything he ever wanted, yet he did not want it anymore. There really were no grounds for breaking off this new marriage.

I remember talking to him over the phone and explaining that it was the Devil putting those feelings into him, so that he would continue the legacy of divorce in his family line. I encouraged him that through prayer and resisting the generational curse, he could beat this and receive generational blessing. One of Eder's good characteristics is that he is humble and willing to listen. So, we prayed and he decided to give it another chance. After a few months I received news that things were getting better, and they were enjoying a happy marriage.

Shortly after, Eder and Tatiana moved to the Tri-Cities, and they surrendered and recommitted their lives to Jesus. Then they decided to get baptized. As they struggled to fit into this new community and find work, feelings of separating returned, and the thought of moving back to his native country invaded Eder's mind. We decided to meet at a local Starbucks, and I explained that the Devil was throwing his last shot to make divorce a part of his life. I reassured him that he is free from that, but as Pharaoh came back and attacked Israel three days after they walked out of Egypt, so it was now, the Devil throwing his last shot at Eder and Tatiana's union. The Israelites did not give in, nor did they go back to Egypt to get delivered again. Instead, they went forward and God drowned Pharaoh and his army in the sea.

Prophetically speaking, I felt that if Eder did not give in to those feelings of separation, then those feelings would stop permanently. We prayed and went our separate ways. It has been over six years since that meeting. Now, they are expecting their third child. Since then, he has found a great passion for photography. These two individuals, Eder and Tatiana, are deeply in love, and are a great example to many other couples, to show that your history does not define your destiny.

Curses are Real

The truth about curses is disbelieved by a large majority of evangelical Christians in America. On the other hand, the reaction of those living in the Caribbean, South and Central America, Africa, India, Asia, and the Far East, is very different. For hundreds of years the United States has enjoyed the benefits of Christian culture. As a result, we do not need much deliverance from the occult or idolatry. However, this is changing because of the rise of false religions in America.

When Adam and Eve sinned, it brought a curse on child-bearing and a curse on the ground (see Genesis 3:17-18). Their first child murdered his younger brother, which also resulted in a curse (see Genesis 4:11:16). When Noah's son dishonored his father, a curse also followed (see Genesis 9:24-27). This pattern of curses continues throughout the Old Testament.

It is clear to see that breaking God's commandments brings a curse, and obeying God brings a blessing. If you believe in blessing, then you already understand the existence of curses.

To be blessed means to be empowered for expansion. God blessed the first parents, Adam and Eve; He also blessed Noah, and Abraham. Jesus blessed the disciples before going up to Heaven, because blessing is empowerment.

One of the best illustrations is observed in the life of Jesus. When Jesus blessed the few loaves that were handed to Him, they were multiplied; but when He cursed the fig tree, it withered (see Matthew 14:19, 21:19). Therefore, whatever is blessed multiplies, and whatever is cursed withers away. Blessing pushes you forward, while a curse is a force that holds you back. Chapter 28 of Deuteronomy lists all the major blessings and curses that can come upon you and overtake you. There are chronic sicknesses, fears and phobias, negative family cycles, premature deaths, constant lack and poverty, accident proneness, divorce, and barrenness.

Jesus came to die on the cross for all our sins. Yet, not just for our sin, but also to remove the power and consequences of those sins. This is why His stripes hold the power to heal any sickness. By dying on the cross, He removed the power of the curse. He could have died from being stoned, being beheaded, or any other means.

However, God chose to resolve the issue of the curse by His crucifixion.

It is written, "Cursed is everyone who hangs on a tree," (see Galatians 3:13). Freedom from curses has been included in the finished work and redemption of the cross. When we got saved, this freedom was also promised to us. As with all of God's benefits through Calvary, we must possess them, not merely profess that they belong to us. God gave the Promised Land to Israel, but they did not live in it until they possessed what they were promised. The same applies to our Promised Land of victory over sin, curse, and demons.

Alive but Bound

The resurrection of Lazarus beautifully portrays this picture of the removal of curses. Lazarus was a good friend of Jesus, who got sick and died. Sin works in like manner and it does not make us bad people, in fact, it does something worse, it makes us dead people. Nevertheless, Jesus came on the scene and spoke a word that raised Lazarus from the dead. Likewise, salvation only comes through Jesus and moves us from death to life. Lazarus was dead and bound with grave clothes, and his face wrapped with a cloth. Jesus said, "…'Loose him, and let him go,'" (John 11:44). In other words, Lazarus was alive, but bound with grave clothes.

When we spiritually die, it signifies that our enemy has bound us. It is an easy task for him to bind dead people, but it is nearly impossible for him to bind living people. The best way to avoid curses is to stay as close as possible to Holy Spirit. This is why the hardest target to hit is a moving target. These grave clothes covered his hands, feet, and face. Remember, Lazarus was alive, but bound in his walking (feet), working (hands), seeing and hearing (face). The Devil likes to bind our feet, so that we do not run after God. He also seeks to put a chain on our hands, so that we do not lift them in prayer and worship to our Savior. The enemy also binds our face, so that we do not see God, hear God, nor taste His wonderful presence.

When you are bound, it does not necessarily mean you are dead; it simply means you are restricted. There are times during a church service that I demonstrate this principle by taking duct tape and slowly taping a person's ears, eyes, hands, and feet. Then I ask the bound person to try to walk. Everyone laughs, of course, because that person cannot see where he is walking. Then when that person tries to run, he cannot; so instead, he attempts to jump. If that person is not careful, he can easily fall and hurt himself. I, then, tell the audience that this person represents a bound Christian, who is indeed alive, but restricted. This type of Christian lacks consistency. One may think that if someone is truly born again, then that individual would not have this type of problem.

Lazarus was truly alive, yet he was bound. Maybe you are like Lazarus, you have been born again, but you still carry signs of grave clothes, past trauma, and chronic sicknesses passed on to you from one generation to another. It seems like everyone in your family line gets divorced, there are constant shortages of finances, you are accident prone, or a black cloud seems to follow you everywhere you go that withholds all of God's blessings. Jesus commanded His followers to loosen Lazarus, which I am glad they did.

Likewise, this book is an assignment from the Lord to help you find freedom in His name. Before we jump into that, let's take a look at three types of grave clothes the Devil uses to hold people back and limit their potential.

Generational Curses

Generational curses are passed down through the generations, with the same recurring problems and troubles that all of our previous ancestors experienced. The Bible describes it as "iniquity of the fathers" (see Numbers 14:18). For example, Abraham had a father who worshipped idols (see Joshua 24:2). Coming from a past of occultic practices, Abraham faced some issues; one of them was fear and lying—he lied about his wife. Abraham's son, Isaac, lied about his wife as well. Then Abraham's grandson lied about his birthright, and his great grandchildren lied about what happened to Joseph. Furthermore, lying was not the only generational issue that was passed on, many of their wives were afflicted with barrenness.

When we are born, many traits get passed down from our parents through their genetics. For example, the color of our hair, the color of our eyes, our skin tone, and many other physical features. Moreover, character traits also get passed on to the next generation. Statistics confirm that we are 10 times more likely to drink if our parents were alcoholics.

We inherit bad traits through our parents' genes, but they lay dormant and are activated by our choices and associations. This principle applies to both generational blessings and generational curses. Although, certain traits and tendencies are passed on through our parents' genes, it does not mean they have to be activated. Negative experiences, bad company, and wrong choices are what activate negative genetic traits. When we surround ourselves with believers, fill our minds with the Word of God and make choices that honor the Lord, then negative things that are inherited by our parents will not be activated.

We must understand that we will not carry the punishment for our ancestor's choices (see Ezekiel 18:2).

Two Families: Edwards and Jukes

There was a study conducted by A.E. Winship, about two families — one descending from Jonathan Edwards and the other from Max Jukes. Winship was visiting state prisons and met criminals who were descendants from the family of Max Jukes. After looking up their records, reports, and testimonies, he learned Max Jukes, an atheist, lived a godless life. He married an ungodly girl, and from that union there were 310 progeny who died as paupers, 150 were criminals, seven were murderers, 100 were drunkards, and more than half of the women were prostitutes. His 540 descendants cost the State $1,250,000.

Sometime later, A.E. Winship was asked to prepare a paper on Jonathan Edwards, who was a puritan preacher and had 11 children with his wife. Winship discovered that the Edwards family line produced the following achievers: one became a U.S. vice-president, three were U.S. senators, three were governors, three were mayors, 13 were college presidents, 30 were judges, 65 were professors, 80 held public offices, 100 were lawyers, and 100 were in the ministry — missionaries, pastors and theologians. One does not have to be a rocket scientist to see that there is a big contrast between these two families.[4]

"The curse of the Lord is on the house of the wicked," (Proverbs 3:33). It is not just on the wicked that the curse comes upon, but on the entire house of the wicked. These curses will continue from one generation to another—until someone faces them and puts an end to them.

The Kennedy Curse

The Kennedy curse is a term used to describe a series of unfortunate events that happened to members of the American Kennedy family. Some critics claim that this is a normal experience

51

for most families. Nevertheless, Senator Edward "Ted" Kennedy, actually wondered out loud if his family were victims of an "awful curse" — as if a curse can be real.[5]

The following outlines the Kennedy Curse:[6]

1941 — Rosemary Kennedy experienced mood swings, which were a sign of a mental disability. Her father — afraid the Kennedy reputation would be ruined—set up a private surgical lobotomy which left her unable to speak or walk. Shortly afterwards, she was put into an institution and she remained there until her death in 2005.

August 12, 1944 — Joseph P. Kennedy Jr. died in an airplane explosion, in England, during World War II.

May 13, 1948 — Kathleen Cavendish, Marchioness of Hartington died in an airplane crash in France.

August 9, 1963 — Patrick Bouvier Kennedy was born premature and died two days later due to a respiratory syndrome.

November 22, 1963 — U.S. President John F. Kennedy was assassinated in Texas.

June 19, 1964 — U.S. Senator Ted Kennedy was involved in an airplane crash where two people, including the pilot, were killed. He was saved — by being pulled out of the aircraft — by another senator and was hospitalized; to recover from severe broken bones, internal bleeding, and a punctured lung.

June 5, 1968 — U.S. Senator Robert F. Kennedy was assassinated in Los Angeles by Sirhan Sirhan, right after his victory for candidacy for president.

July 18, 1969 — Ted Kennedy accidently drove his vehicle off a bridge in Chappaquiddick Island. His passenger, Mary Jo Kopechne, was left trapped in the vehicle; and he left and felt guilty for departing the scene without saving her. Shortly afterwards, during a television broadcast, Ted said that during that night he wondered "whether some awful curse actually did hang over all the Kennedys."

August 13, 1973 — Joseph P. Kennedy II crashed while driving a Jeep, leaving the passenger paralyzed.

April 25, 1984 — David A. Kennedy died due to an overdose of cocaine and pethidine in a hotel room in Florida.

April 1, 1991 — William Kennedy Smith raped a young woman in the Kennedy estate property in Florida; he was arrested and charged for the crime. However, due to media involvement, Smith was declared innocent.

December 31, 1997 — Michael LeMoyne Kennedy died in a skiing accident in Colorado.

July 16, 1999 — John F. Kennedy Jr. — who was the pilot in his own plane — died in a plane crash over the Atlantic Ocean, which also killed his wife and sister-in-law.

September 16, 2011 — Kara Kennedy had a heart attack while doing physical exercises at a health club at age 51. Furthermore, she had suffered from lung cancer nine years prior; which resulted in part of her right lung being removed.

May 16, 2012 — Mary Richardson Kennedy committed suicide in her home in New York.

It is clear to see that these terrible accidents and premature deaths were not normal. The Bible reveals to us that these are signs of generational curses. However, as we have discovered, being rich and famous will not stop curses; only Jesus holds the power to break these curses.

Dealing with Daddy's Enemies

Many years ago, I purchased a rundown rental property, to create passive income. The property was not managed well by the previous owners. The house needed renovation and the land required a lot of work. There wasn't any grass, only weeds. The weeds were not planted by me, and I grew frustrated seeing all those weeds and no grass. The previous owner left a lot work to do. Instead of blaming the previous owner for not doing his job, I, slowly but surely, applied lawn care chemicals to kill the weeds, which caused the grass to flourish. By the time the property was sold, the lawn was green and abundant. I passed on a very beautiful lawn to the next owner.

Maybe you had parents who did not deal with some issues, and consequently, these issues got passed onto you. Scripture does not tell us to blame others, but to resist the Devil and deal with the root of the issue.

When Solomon inherited the throne from his dad, King David, he also inherited some enemies his father did not deal with. I really love how David warned Solomon regarding those enemies, however, Solomon still had to deal with the enemies. King David died, but his enemies were still around and caused problems for Solomon.

Demons and curses do not die with people; instead, they continue to afflict the succeeding generations. Solomon knew that before he could establish his kingdom, he had to remove his daddy's "demons." Unfortunately, not all of us are privileged to have parents that are transparent enough to inform us of certain bad habits and traits. Thus, we will have to confront these enemies in our own lives, because they were not dealt with by our parents. Solomon — considered the wisest man on earth — makes it his first priority to deal with his father's adversaries, before building the temple in his kingdom. As a result, King Solomon exiled some and executed others, as the Scriptures confirm, "…thus the kingdom was established in the hand of Solomon," (1 Kings 2:46).

When you execute and exile generational curses, you will then establish yourself in the blessings of God.

Cast Curses

Generational curses are passed down, but cast curses are spoken over. The power of life and death is in our tongue (see Proverbs 18:21). Hence, words are the vehicle for curses and blessings.

Now, who is able to speak these curses? We know God pronounced a curse on the serpent and on the ground (see Genesis 3:14; 3:17; 5:29). God promised to curse those who cursed Abraham (see Genesis 12:3). We also learned, in previous chapters, that practicing the occult is the main reason God pronounces a curse on an individual.

However, not only God, but also men of God, can pronounce a curse. For example, Joshua cursed Jericho, King David cursed the Mountain of Gilboa, the Prophet Elisha cursed his servant, and Jesus cursed the fig tree (see Joshua 6:26; 2 Samuel 2:21; 2 Kings 5:26-27).

Men of God have an enormous responsibility to bless people, and not to curse them. We may be tempted to reason that because Elisha and Joshua cursed others, then we should do the same—not true. When the disciples of Jesus wanted to burn the city of Samaria, they used Elijah as a Scriptural reference for destruction. Jesus responded to them with the following, "He turned and rebuked them, and said, 'You do not know what manner of spirit you are of,'" (Luke 9:55). The reality is that the Spirit of Christ always desires to bless people.

I remember praying over this certain lady, who attended a church where the pastor said to her if anyone left his church, their children would go to the world. This lady left his church and all her children, indeed, began to go into the world. She came to pray against those words, which she believed had affected her family. Our only obligation, as ministers of God, should be to curse all sickness, demons, and evil works of darkness—but never ever should we curse people.

Not only do men of God have power to pronounce curses, but those in authority hold the same power. Parents have this power over their children, and husbands have this power over their wives. Fathers have a huge power in the spiritual world, which can be exercised by speaking either a blessing or curse over their children. Noah was a well-known father, who cursed his son, Ham, for a mistake he committed. That curse has affected the generations after Ham.

Nobody is perfect, but speaking blessing over people helps them become perfected. When people make mistakes, commit sin, break our trust, or hurt us deeply, we have a decision to make—whether to release evil forces or release blessing their way by our words. Words such as, "You are worthless," "You are stupid," "You never amount to anything," "Why can't you be more like so and so," "You are fat," "You are ugly," and "I wish you were dead," may seem like nothing, but the Devil seeks and grabs onto what he can attach to in order to bring evil into people's lives.

I was speaking at a camp and a young man came up for prayer. He struggled with getting good grades and his mom would always say, "You are slow" or "You are so stupid." With tears rolling down his eyes, he confessed that these words became like a chain that limited his academic progress. We prayed, renounced, and replaced those words with positive ones. I spoke the opposite over him and blessed him as a father figure.

Another source of "cast curses" are servants of the Devil—witches and witch doctors. Witch doctors cast spells on those they want to harm. That is why, in the Bible, Balak hired Balaam to pronounce a curse on Israel, so that they would be defeated in battle. We are not to be afraid of any spells or curses cast by the servants of Satan.

I have heard so many confessions and testimonies of people, who, out of jealousy, hire a witch to cast a spell to cause unfortunate things to come upon their enemies. The main problem is that the spell they cast on their enemy, usually comes back on them. Thus, as Christians we should not be afraid of the Devil and his spells.

"A curse without cause shall not alight," (Proverbs 26:2 NASB). Matthew Henry shared his perspective through one of his commentaries, "He that is cursed without cause, whether by furious imprecations or solemn anathemas, the curse shall do him no more harm than the bird that flies over his head, or than Goliath's curses did to David. It will fly away like the sparrow or the wild dove, which go nobody knows where, till they return to their proper place, as the curse will at length return upon the head of him that uttered it."[7] If we are serving God, then God will protect us — even when we do not realize it.

When You Cast a Curse on Yourself

The last source for "cast curses" is ourselves. This is when curses are self-imposed. Things we always speak about, and to, ourselves can become our own prison.

God protected the children of Abraham from the curses of others, but not from their own. The Jewish people also claimed a self-imposed curse (see Matthew 27:24-25).

One of the many reasons I do not swear is because swearing pronounces a curse. When we swear, we release curses. We must repent and not speak self-imposed curses on ourselves, and replace them with God's Word and thoughts about us. For example, when we are sick we must align ourselves with God's Word and declare, "I will not die, but live," (see Psalm 118:17). Also, when we are weak, proclaim, "I am strong" and "I am more than a conqueror through Jesus," (see Joel 3:10; Romans 8:37).

I am not suggesting that we deny that our problems exist, but it is vital that we do not give our problems a place that will influence and impact us negatively. For example, when I feel sick I like to say, "I am not a sick person trying to get healthier, I am a healthy person fighting sickness." If you are fighting sinful tendencies in your life, then say the following, "I am not a sinner trying to get holy, I am a righteous person fighting sin."

God wants us to repent of all negative words that we have spoken over ourselves, and replace them with positive declarations from His Word. When Peter denied Jesus three times, Jesus not only forgave him, but also reversed the power of those words by having Peter speak the opposite three times.

Earned Curses

As I mentioned previously, generational curses are passed on from preceding generations. On the other hand, "cast curses" are spoken words by others or ourselves. However, "earned curses" are when the law of sowing and reaping activates in our lives. The curse of Jotham is an example of that (see Judges 9). When his brother Abimelech killed his 70 brothers without any cause and the city of Shechem embraced this murderer as their leader, Jotham cursed Abimelech and the city of Shechem. The city and its new leader enjoyed temporary blessing for three years, but then problems began. "God sent a spirit of ill will between Abimelech and the men of Shechem; and the men of Shechem dealt treacherously with Abimelech." (Judges 9:23).

The spirit of ill always comes wherever there is a curse. These spirits always cause strife and problems which eventually lead to destruction. As a consequence, a shameful death came to Abimelech because he reaped what he sowed. "And all the evil of the men of Shechem God returned on their own heads, and on them came the curse of Jotham the son of Jerubbaal," (Judges 9:57). As we can see, spiritual forces stood behind all of these calamities that came upon Abimelech and the city of Shechem. Dark spiritual forces always bring curses.

The Six Biblical Causes for Earned Curses

1. Worshipping idols (see Deuteronomy 27:15). As we already learned, idolatry, the occult, and witchcraft are open doors for curses.

2. Disrespect for parents (see Deuteronomy 27:16). Out of all the 10 commandments, the only one that carries a blessing is the commandment of honoring our father and mother. If a blessing is attached to honoring parents, then be certain that dishonoring parents brings a curse. I always advise teenagers, "If you want to live long and have a healthy life, honor your mom and dad." This commandment is more important than your education and connections.

3. Injustice to the weak and helpless (see Deuteronomy 27:18-19). When we commit injustice against others, it also brings a curse. Cain was under a curse after he murdered his brother (see Genesis 4:11-12). Abortion is murder, and it brings a curse. I have previously ministered to people, who became possessed by demons after committing the act of abortion. When we take someone's life or bring deep pain to someone — especially when they are helpless or less fortunate—it opens our lives to all kinds of trouble.

4. Illicit behavior, unnatural sex, and incest (see Deuteronomy 27:20-23). Sex is not just a physical act, it is a spiritual matter as well. An individual becomes one with another individual the moment they have sex (see 1 Corinthians 6:16). Condoms can protect from sexual disease, but not from sexual demons. Demons can be transferred from one person to another through a sexual act. I have heard plenty of testimonies of people—who were in the kingdom of darkness—that were assigned by the devil to recruit as many people as possible by having sex with them. Protection from demonic assaults on our life is one of the many benefits of living a pure and holy lifestyle, and preserving sex for marriage.

5. Anti-Semitism (see Genesis 12:3). Powerful empires who attacked the Jewish people, and tried to wipe them out from our planet, paid dearly. God promises that those who try to curse Israel will be cursed. We all know Adolf Hitler, the leader of Nazi Germany—who was obsessed with destroying the Jews—he and his regime had a terrible end. Today, many in the Arab world continue this wicked legacy. Even though the Arab world has plenty of oil and money, they still carry curses. As Bret Stephens of the Wall Street Journal said, "Today, there is no great university in the Arab world, no serious indigenous scientific base, a stunted literary culture. In 2015 the US Patent Office reported 3,804 patents from Israel, as compared with 364 from Saudi Arabia, 56 from the United Arab Emirates, and 30 from Egypt."[8] Also, let us not forget every writer from the Bible was Jewish, and our very Savior came from the Jewish nation. He is the soon coming King, Who will sit on David's throne. We need to continue to pray for peace in Jerusalem, and God's blessing will be released in our lives.

6. Stealing and perjury. "'I will send out the curse,' says the Lord of hosts; 'It shall enter the house of the thief and the house of the one who swears falsely by My name. It shall remain in the midst of his house and consume it, with its timber and stones,'" (Zechariah 5:4). Stealing is a sin because it breaks one of God's commandments. It also opens doors for curses upon our household. Judas was a disciple of Jesus, yet he was a thief. Thievery led to demonic possession, and to Judas' eventual destruction. When we have people who work for us, and we do not pay a fair wage, but grow rich from their labor, then a curse will enter our house and consume our lives. Robbery, burglary, identity theft, stealing from the office, taking intellectual property — illegally downloading content and shoplifting, are acts of sowing, which will result in reaping many curses.

Those who stole, for example, Achan, Gehazi, Judas, and the thieves on the cross, all suffered a curse for their actions — but Jesus wants to forgive thieves and break the power of this curse on their lives. Jesus was crucified between two thieves, one who had the curse broken and received salvation, and one who kept his curse and died without breaking the curse over his life. When Zacchaeus found salvation, he promised to pay back the people he had hurt financially. Jesus did not stop him. In fact, He said, "Today salvation has come to this house, because he also is a son of Abraham," (Luke 19:9).

If we want to break the curses on our finances due to stealing, we need to apologize and make restitution with those who we have hurt along the way. I have had people on our team who had stolen things from stores and other people, and as a result, they had perpetual financial problems. One time during prayer and fasting, Holy Spirit convicted these members of my team, so they apologized to the people they stole from and made amends. It was embarrassing for them, but something changed when they acted just as Zacchaeus did. Because of this, God's blessing was poured over their finances and their financial circumstances improved.

Furthermore, stealing is not only limited to taking what does not belong to us, but also withholding our tithe. "You are cursed with a curse, for you have robbed Me, even this whole nation," (Malachi 3:9). When we withhold our tithe, we open our finances to a curse. We rob God and do not provide Him the opportunity to bless us.

Prayer

"Father God, I come to You with a heart full of thanksgiving for sending Jesus to die on the cross for my sin. By His death, You have now rendered all curses formed against me, powerless. I repent for the sins of my ancestors who did not serve You, but instead served the devil. I repent for anything I repeatedly spoke over myself that does not line up with your Word. I repent of any heart break I have caused my parents. Remove any, and all, rebellion in my heart. Forgive me for anytime I have failed to help those in need, when it was in my power to do so. Anything I have stolen, I repent of today, and I promise not to do it again. Any curse that came because of these things, let it be broken today by the power of Jesus' blood. Anything evil that has been passed on in my DNA through my family, I break it, in Jesus' name. I break any words of death spoken over me by those in authority. I cancel any spells by witchdoctors. No weapon formed against me will prosper, in Jesus' name. Holy Spirit help me to walk in the blessings of God and pass them onto the next generation."

CHAPTER 5

THE CHILDREN'S BREAD

A long time ago, there was a story of a minister who was immigrating to the US on a ship. This voyage lasted 21 days. He sold everything he had to buy a ticket, but did not have enough money for expensive food on the ship. Instead, he brought a big bag of cheese and crackers. Every day as people would go to the cafeteria to eat, he would go to the deck with his cheese and crackers to eat there. Hearing the laugher of those in the cafeteria, this poor traveler reminded himself that, although he did not have access to the fancy food, he was at least on his way to America. On the last day, one gentleman approached this minister and asked why he did not join everyone in the cafeteria. He was embarrassed and replied that he was too poor to go there. His new friend replied, "The food in all of the buffets and restaurants was included in your ticket."

We, who are believers in Jesus, are all on our way to Heaven. Jesus purchased that ticket for us by His death on the cross. There are other blessings included in salvation. Salvation is more than just a ticket to heaven, it is a door to the green pastures of life in the kingdom.

Salvation in Three Tenses

Our spirit is saved during the time of conversion, our soul is saved through sanctification, and our body will be saved at the time of resurrection. As believers, we have been saved, we are currently being saved, and we shall be saved in the future.

First, we see that a Christian has already been saved by transferring from the kingdom of darkness to the kingdom of Christ, passing from death to life. "For by grace you have been saved through faith..." (Ephesians 2:8).

Second, we are in the process of being saved. Paul spoke to the Corinthians as "...those who are being saved," (2 Corinthians 2:15). He also told the Philippians, "...work out your own salvation with fear and trembling, for it is God who works in you..." (Philippians 2:12-13). This salvation happens in our soul, where Holy Spirit brings renewal to our mind, healing to our emotions, and freedom to our will. Our soul is the part that is being saved while we are on this earth.

Third, the future portion of our salvation is mentioned twice by Paul, "...we shall be saved..." (Romans 5:9-10). This is neither in the past, nor present tense. It is part of our future. Paul also made an interesting statement, "Our salvation is now nearer than when we first believed," (Romans 13:11). This is when we will experience being in a new body through the resurrection.

As you see, salvation is not just an event but a process. Salvation in the present tense is where the renewing of the mind, healing of the soul, crucifying of our flesh, and deliverance takes place.

Can Christians have Demons?

When a Christian is delivered from demons or curses, it does not mean that those spirits lived in his spirit. Holy Spirit occupies the spirit of the believer, but demons can harass, torment, and oppress the soul of the believer. Holy Spirit possesses the believer, meaning He owns him. Demonic spirits seek to oppress the Christian by controlling a part of his life. Being tormented by demons does not mean that you are not saved. It does not mean that those spirits own you.

Derek Prince, who is a powerful influence on my life in the area of deliverance, shared in one of his talks that the Greek word New Testament writers used for demonic possession is "demonized." He would explain that being demonized does not mean ownership, but partial control. It means that demons seek to control one area of your life. They cannot have possession or ownership of your spirit. How do you know which area demons control? Usually it is in the areas where you do not have control, because some demon is controlling that area of your soul. When you get delivered, you get the control back. During deliverance, that part of your soul gets saved.

Maybe you are thinking, darkness and light cannot be together. It does not say that in the Bible. Some think that Holy Spirit and an evil spirit cannot dwell in the same vessel. Really? Says who? The Scripture that we get this from states "Do not be unequally yoked together with unbelievers. For what fellowship has righteousness with lawlessness? And what communion has light with darkness?" (2 Corinthians 6:14). This verse does not say light and darkness cannot coexist. It says they should not exist together. Paul is telling us the way things should be, not what they cannot be.

If you think Christians cannot be demonized, let me tell you, there are stories of when light and darkness operated in the same person. A fallen pastor who once preached holiness while frequently visiting prostitutes; a newly saved believer who habitually returned to drug abuse and suicidal attempts of self-destruction; a Christian leader who influenced many for the Gospel's sake, but ended up in jail for fraud and thievery, are some examples.

Paul stated in 2 Corinthians 6:14, "Do not be unequally yoked together with unbelievers," and then went on talking about how darkness and light should not have any fellowship together. If darkness and light cannot coexist, then Christians cannot date unbelievers. We know that this happens all of the time. It should not, but it does. Same thing happens with demonized Christians. They should not be under this demonic influence, but nowhere in the Bible does it say that this is not possible.

Sozo

We are triune beings and our sin affects our whole person. Sin does not just make our spirit dead, but also brings sickness, poverty, and oppression. It would make sense for salvation to affect the whole person as well.

It is important to keep in mind that the word for salvation in Greek is "sozo." The meaning of the word "sozo" is to save, to deliver, to protect, to preserve and rescue from danger. Sozo is used in Matthew 1:21 when it refers to our sins being forgiven. Sozo is used in Matthew 9:22 when it speaks of the healing of a woman. Sozo is used in Luke 8:36 when it talks about a man being delivered from demons.

You see, salvation, or sozo, is one word used to describe forgiveness of sins, healing of disease, and deliverance from demons. Salvation is more than just a ticket to heaven, it is salvation of the spirit, soul, and body.

Deliverance for Christians

A woman of Canaan, of Syro-Pheonician ethnicity, according to the gospel of Mark, worshipped Jesus and asked Him to heal her daughter. Her child was severely demon-possessed, an indication that the child had supernatural manifestation of demons. How could she know that the child's problems were demonic? Jesus, who is God and knew all, did not dispute the mother's assessment.

In response to her begging, Jesus Christ did nothing. Jesus' disciples wanted to send her away. She was not a Jew, and even worse, she was a pagan. Despite this, she was a persistent woman. Finally, Jesus replied to her, "It is not good to take the children's bread and throw it to the little dogs," (Matthew 15:26).

To Jews, all other races and ethnicities were like "dogs," because dogs were identified as despised creatures. She did not give up. Even after hearing that answer, she responded, "Yes, Lord; but even the dogs feed on the crumbs which fall from their masters' table," (Matthew 15:27, NASB). As much as the Jews despised dogs, they brushed the final crumbs of a meal onto the floor for the dogs to eat. That is what she wanted. She was willing to eat the spiritual crumbs, in order for her daughter to be delivered. Moved by her faith, Jesus spoke the word and her daughter was delivered, though physically He was not present next to her.

She got the crumbs, but those who are the children of God get the bread. Not the crumbs, but the full meal of the Gospel which includes deliverance and healing. From Jesus' perspective, deliverance for the believers is what bread is to the children. To say that we do not need to be freed, delivered, or victorious is to say that we do not need bread. This is why Jesus taught His disciples to pray, "…our Father who is in heaven…deliver us from the evil one…" (Matthew 6:9-13). We are God's children, yet we are encouraged to ask for deliverance.

The Basis for Deliverance

The cross of Jesus Christ is the basis for our freedom. The message of the cross is the power and wisdom of God (see 1

Corinthians 1:18). On Calvary, Jesus was punished for our sin so that we can be forgiven. He was condemned that we might be justified. Jesus became sin, so that we can become righteous. He died, so that we can live. There was a divine exchange that took place at the cross.

On the cross, Jesus was punished, so that we might be forgiven (see Matthew 9:6). Forgiveness is free for us, but it cost the Father His Son to able to forgive us our sins.

On the cross, Jesus was condemned, so that we might be justified (see Romans 3:24). Sin brings condemnation. Salvation brings freedom from guilt. Jesus took our guilt so that we could be made just – as though we have never sinned before. Forgiveness forgives your sin, but justification makes you innocent – like you never did that sin.

On the cross, Jesus became sin, so that we might become righteous (see 2 Corinthians 5:21). Jesus took your sin to give you His righteousness.

On the cross, Jesus died, so that we might live (see John 10:10; Romans 6:23). Jesus came to give His life to us and take our (spiritual) death upon Himself. What does Jesus' life look like? The original word for "life" in John 10:10 is "zoë" – it is the very life that God has within Himself.

On the cross, Jesus was wounded, so that we might be healed (see Isaiah 53:5). Jesus took a physical beating for our healing. Every sickness was taken upon the body of Jesus.

On the cross, Jesus was cursed, so that we might be blessed (see Galatians 3:13-14). Jesus took generational curses, cast curses, and earned curses, because anyone who hangs on a tree is cursed.' Jesus took our curses, so that we might have blessing.

On the cross, Jesus was poor, so that we might be rich (see 2 Corinthians 8:9). Jesus became poor on the cross: naked, hungry, thirsty, and in need of everything, so that we might be enriched and have more than enough to help our families and spread the kingdom of God with our resources.

On the cross, Jesus was rejected, so that we might be accepted (see Matthew 27:46). Jesus was rejected by God and forsaken by people – He knows how it feels be rejected. We are accepted by God, because Jesus was rejected by Him.

On the cross, Jesus was put to shame, so that we might live in glory (see Matthew 27:35, Hebrews 12:2). Jesus suffered shame, so that we might not walk in shame.

On the cross, Jesus rendered Satan powerless (see Colossians 2:14-15; Genesis 3:15). When Christ died for our sins, Satan was disarmed and defeated. Satan's defeat was prophesied in the Garden of Eden, that Jesus would bruise the head of the serpent.

There are many reasons for demonic oppression, but only one basis for freedom from them, the cross of Calvary. Different sins open the door for the Devil, but only the precious blood of Jesus drives him out. Only the blood of Jesus can overcome the Devil (see Revelation 12:11).

Fight from Victory

Because of the cross and blood of Jesus, the Devil has suffered ultimate defeat already. Victory is paid for. This victory from demons and curses is promised to all believers. Why, then, are so many believers living in defeat? God promised the land of Canaan to all Israel, but only a few occupied it. The children of Abraham possessed only what they fought for, not what God had promised. You do not get what you are promised, you get what you fight for.

"This charge I commit to you, son Timothy, according to the prophecies previously made concerning you, that by them you may wage the good warfare," (1 Timothy 1:18). Many people get prophetic words and do not see them come to pass for the reason that they do not wage warfare from the position of that prophetic word. The promise of God, a prophetic word, or what Jesus has paid for on Calvary has to be received by our faith.

We have to move from merely professing what Jesus did for us on the cross to possessing what He did. Victory on the cross does not remove fighting, instead, it empowers it. Since the days of John the Baptist, the Kingdom of God is taken by force (see Matthew 11:12). You cannot sit on the sidelines and play the victim. The cross made you victorious. You get to rise up and possess what is yours already. Drive away all the forces of the Devil.

More than Conquerors

Every conqueror gets victory after the battle. We get victory before the battle, therefore, we are more than conquerors (see Romans 8:37). When you become a Christian, Jesus gives you authority and the power of Holy Spirit. You are like a policeman in the spiritual world. A police officer has a badge which gives him authority, and a weapon which provides power to back up that authority. Criminals are afraid of officers, because of the authority and the power they carry. When you recognize that the authority and power has already been given to you over the Devil, the enemy panics. He is the criminal, you are the officer. You have the power of heaven backing you up.

We do not fight for victory, we fight from the position of victory. In the famous passage about spiritual warfare in Ephesians 6, Paul says to put on the armor of God "to stand" (see Ephesians 6:11, 13-14). The goal of our spiritual armor is not to get victory, but to stand in the victory that has already been won for us.

Dead Snakes Can be Dangerous

The Bible compares the Devil to five animals:

A bird. He steals the word. (See Matthew 13:4)

A wolf. He snatches and scatters the sheep. (See John 10:12)

A lion. He is not a lion because there is only one true lion – the Lion of the Tribe of Judah. The Devil acts like a lion by roaring and seeking to devour. (See 1 Peter 5:8)

A dragon. He deceives the whole world. (See Revelation 12:9; 20:2)

A serpent or a snake. We first meet Satan in the Bible as a snake. Snakes attack with their mouth and inject poison into their victim. (See Genesis 3:1)

A Medical Center in Phoenix Arizona did a study on rattlesnakes and found that dead rattlesnakes can still strike, bite, and kill. Sometimes rattlesnakes were shot and their heads cut off, but the snake heads still retained the capacity for reflex action. One study showed that snake heads could still make striking type motions for up to 60 minutes after decapitation.[9] Dead snakes are dangerous.

Satan's defeat gives you a potential of victory, but it does not make you an automatic overcomer. Otherwise all believers would be victorious all the time and we would not be commanded to wage war against the Devil and resist our enemy.

Many believers are professing that the Devil is defeated, he is no longer a problem, yet they are also defeated in their own lives. The New Testament authors knew of the defeat of the Devil, yet they admonished, "...nor give place to the devil," (Ephesians 4:27), "...trample on serpents and scorpions..." (Luke 10:19), "...Resist the devil..." (James 4:7), "Be sober, be vigilant; because your adversary the devil walks about like a roaring lion, seeking whom he may devour. Resist him, steadfast in the faith..." (1 Peter 5:8,9).

All this shows that we must be vigilant and sober-minded toward our defeated foe, otherwise we will only profess victory and never possess it. Life is not a playground, it is a battlefield.

Prisoner Turned into a Pet

The case with Samson teaches us a lesson. The Philistines subdued Samson after a long trial. They defeated, blinded, and bound him. They captured him and he became their prisoner. The Philistines started to party and entertain themselves with their captured enemy. Samson was defeated after all, what could he do? Yet he was still dangerous and he was still their enemy. Very soon, his defeat also became their defeat. He took his vengeance on them and was successful because they were not on guard, they treated life as a party and their enemy as a pet. For us to not share the same fate as our enemy, we must acknowledge that he has been disarmed on Calvary. He has been defeated, yet he remains our real enemy and we should never take this lightly.

That is why Peter said to be sober. Paul said to put on the whole armor of God to stand against a defeated foe. If you do not take your defeated enemy seriously, do not be surprised if your life begins to reflect more defeat than victory.

Goliath is Down, Now it is Time to Fight

When David killed Goliath, the enemy fled, but the war was not over, it had only begun. The people of Israel, who were previously hiding from the enemy, now were empowered by David's glorious victory. They found courage in His victory. His victory became their source of strength. David's victory did not cause them to sit and relax, but to fight.

Jesus is a replication of David. He defeated Goliath – the ruler of darkness. Goliath is down. Now, let's rise and fight. Get your purity back. Get your freedom back. Your enemy is already fleeing, he is in panic. Do not let him get away with anything. You have the badge of God's authority, and the power of Holy Spirit to make the victory from Calvary a reality in your life.

Prayer

"I praise You, God, my Father, because You blessed me in the heavenly places with every spiritual blessing in Jesus Christ. I thank You, Jesus, my Savior, for giving me the greatest gift of salvation and new life. I welcome You, Holy Spirit, to reveal to me the riches of my inheritance in Christ. I will not live by just professing my promised land, but possessing it in Jesus' name."

CHAPTER 6

FIND FREEDOM

John was diagnosed by doctors with uncontrollable and intrusive thoughts, a tick disorder, panic disorder, insomnia, and suicidal tendencies. He had these terrible disorders for three years. The intrusive thoughts were so horrific that he said it was like having another person live inside of him and think for him. Uncontrollable thoughts would come into his mind to curse God, and to curse his family, so they would die. It became so severe that he stopped going to school, when, previously, he had been an "A" student. His disorders would cause him to have a hard time determining which multiple-choice answers to select on an assignment. A tick disorder developed—as a coping mechanism—to combat those tormenting thoughts. Furthermore, he would hit his own body to stop those intrusive thoughts.

I remember seeing him for the first time at one of our services. His body was twisted as he slapped his head with his hand. John had a very difficult time resting and sleeping. He had to watch movies or shows on television to drown out the intrusive thoughts, so he could get sleep. Because of his many suicide attempts, he ended up in a mental institution where he was put on medicine to numb what he was experiencing. His family then began to look for help elsewhere. They tried alternative medicine, natural vitamins, and prayers from churches, all to no avail.

His parents finally brought him to our monthly prayer line, where we pray for deliverance. As I was praying for him, Holy Spirit began to remove all the evil that was plaguing him. He began to manifest and threw up all kinds of nasty substances. After the deliverance, he went back home, and that same day he stopped taking Benadryl, which he usually took every two hours to help him sleep. Also, the intrusive and suicidal thoughts were gone from his mind. His mind was restored and he was able to make decisions. John was able to test again and finish his GED. God completely restored his life. He then came back to testify for the glory of Jesus. Today, he is a leader at a local church, leading youth to Jesus. Glory to God!

Identify the Enemy

The first step to finding freedom is to recognize you are in need of freedom. Identifying your enemy is 50 percent of the victory. It may seem like a no-brainer, however, bondage is very deceptive. Many people who are bound, think they are free. Jesus told the Jews, who believed in Him, that if they abide in His Word, then they will be His disciples indeed — and the truth will set them free. Their response was like many today, "We do not need to be free — we are Abraham's descendants." This sounds very similar to what many Christians say today — "We do not need deliverance, we are fine." Jesus' new followers actually replied that they had never been in bondage to anyone (see John 8:31-36). That was a bold statement — but were they really never in bondage to anyone? History shows that the Jews have been in bondage to many; including the Egyptians, Midianites, Philistines, Babylonians, and at that time, the Romans. How could they say that they had never been in bondage?

It is evident, that bondage is very deceptive. In order to be free, you must realize that you are not free. You must recognize your need for freedom and be desperate for it. Derek Prince used to say, "The Holy Spirit is for the thirsty, but deliverance is for the desperate." Jesus also explained to His disciples why it was important to continue in His Word — to become and remain free.

Jesus declared, "Most assuredly, I say to you, whoever commits sin is a slave of sin. And a slave does not abide in the house forever, but a son abides forever," (John 8:34-35).

One can be a disciple of Jesus and still commit the same sin time after time. When we fall into habitual sin it becomes bondage - it is being a slave to that sin. I did not come up with that, Jesus did! Also, remember that He was addressing His new followers. Habitual sinning or being a slave of any sin has a price attached to it — one will not abide in the house forever. This means one will not remain consistent in his relationship with God, nor in his purpose in the Church.

One of the main reasons people do not stay in church is because they are not free. The bondage they carry does not allow them to stay in the house forever. Now, the opposite of slavery is sonship. Sonship is more than just being a child of God; it signifies being free from the grip of sin and led by the Spirit of God. When you take notice that you keep falling into the same sin, or the same unfortunate things happen, then it is a sign that you need freedom. Jesus is that truth, and He is the source of that freedom.

Confess Sins

After we recognize our need for freedom, we must repent from our sins and the sins of our forefathers. Confessing our sin opens the doors for us to experience God's freedom. Repenting of our sins also closes all the doors to demons. It is important for us to submit to Holy Spirit, so He can lead us to repentance. Do not go to your past and try to find every sin you have committed. Instead, let the Spirit of God bring to memory all the things you must repent of, and those doors will be closed. There are obvious sins that we need to turn away from, but many times, we do not know which particular sin actually opened the door to the enemy.

When there was famine for three consecutive years, David asked God why this was happening. Then God revealed that Saul had broken the treaty with the Gibeonites (see 2 Samuel 21:1). Contrariwise, David took the right steps to undo what Saul had caused, and the famine was stopped. In this particular case, it was not David's sin that caused the famine, but it was the sin of his predecessor—King Saul.

There are times we need to repent for the sins of our forefathers. "And those of you who are left shall waste away in their iniquity in your enemies' lands; also, in their fathers' iniquities, which are with them, they shall waste away. 'But if they confess their iniquity and the iniquity of their fathers, with their unfaithfulness in which they were unfaithful to Me, and that they also have walked contrary to Me," (Leviticus 26:39-40). We confess the sins of our parents, not so they can be forgiven, but so that all access to us by the enemy is denied, all doors are closed, and the grip of the Devil broken.

When it comes to our personal repentance, we must understand that repentance is more than regretting what we have done. Remorse is not repentance. Judas had remorse when he betrayed Jesus, but there was no repentance there. Judas even restored the money back to the Pharisees, but there was no repentance toward God.

Repentance is acknowledging that what we did was wrong before God, even if no one saw it or got hurt by it. It is personally confessing to God that we are sorry. It is willingly choosing to change the direction of our walk. Imagine you are driving one day, and it dawns on you that you are heading in the wrong direction, so you take a U-turn. Repentance is the U-turn, and it is more than just remorse. It is not just settling for relief, and then once our lives get better, we go back to living in our old ways of sin. Too many people are looking for relief from their problem, but are not truly seeking repentance.

In addition to confessing our sins to God, there is power in confessing our sins to a trusted mentor or pastor. The Apostle James said that confession brings healing (see James 5:16). There is deliverance that takes place when you bring your sin out into the open light. This is because sin grows in the dark. When we justify our sin, blame others, and hide in secrecy, we empower the Devil to continue to hold us in bondage. Repentance always breaks that grip!

Surrender to the Lordship of Jesus

There is a story that Evangelist Reinhard Bonnke shared in one of his crusades about a little boy with a big house. This boy had a house with two stories and 10 rooms. The story goes on to say that there was a time when Jesus knocked on the front door and asked to come in. The little boy was honored to have Jesus live inside. He offered Jesus the best room—the master bedroom.

The next day, there was another knock on the door. When the boy opened the door, to see who it was, it was the Devil. The Devil began to push against the door to force himself in. The little boy wrestled with the Devil for a long time and finally pushed him out, and closed the door. Tired from fighting, he rested on the couch, and there was Jesus walking down from his master bedroom. The little boy was disappointed that Jesus did not help him fight the Devil. He asked Jesus, "Why didn't you help me?"

Jesus said, "I am a guest, you are the owner." Then the boy had a revelation! Jesus needs more rooms. Thus, he decided to give Jesus all of upstairs—which was a total of five rooms—but this still left the boy with five rooms for himself. The little boy reasoned that the problem was solved, so he went to sleep.

The next morning, there was again a knock at the door. The little boy was not too excited to open the door. So, instead, he opened it just a bit to see who it was. As he opened the door just a little, the Devil stuck his foot into the opening, and started to wrestle with the little boy to get in. Exhausted from wrestling with the Devil, the boy finally managed to shut the door and kick the Devil out. Then, he quickly ran to Jesus to voice his complaint and said, "Why aren't You helping me? I gave You five rooms. Why am I still fighting the Devil by myself?" Jesus replied, "I am grateful to be a guest in your house with five rooms, but you are the owner, it is your responsibility to answer the door."

Then the light bulb turned on in the little boy's mind! He finally got it! He gave Jesus the keys to the house and said to Him, "You are the owner now, and I am the guest, where would You have me stay?" Jesus gave him the master bedroom to stay in as a guest. The next day there was a knock at the door. The little boy got up to answer the door, but Jesus told him to go back to sleep. Jesus also told him that it was not his duty to answer the door, that he was only a guest. So, Jesus went to answer the door, in the meantime the little boy watched from the corner to see what would happen. When Jesus answered that door, there stood the Devil. Seeing Jesus, he bowed down to his knees and said, "Sir this is the wrong house, I am so sorry." Though it is just a parable, it has a powerful message consistent with the Scriptures.

"Therefore, submit to God. Resist the Devil and he will flee from you," (James 4:7). Before we go rebuking, we must first submit ourselves to God. However, submitting to the Lordship of Jesus is more than just praying the sinner's prayer. Many have received Jesus as their Savior, but have not submitted to Him as their Lord. They are still in charge of their house and still hold the keys. Jesus is willing to take full responsibility for those under His Lordship. When Jesus becomes your Savior and Lord, resisting the Devil will be effectual. It will not just be empty words without power.

It is interesting to see how Judas—being a disciple and friend of Jesus—was able to come under demonic possession. When we read the Gospels, we see Judas calling Jesus a teacher, but never his Lord. To Judas, Jesus was a good teacher and a friend, but not his God. You can be very familiar with God, and even call him your friend, however, the Devil does not care about that. The Devil only responds to authority. If you are not under the authority of Jesus, you cannot walk in the authority of Jesus. I am all for being a friend of God, but our friendship with Him should not be a substitute for complete submission to Him as our Lord.

"Now the Lord is the Spirit; and where the Spirit of the Lord is, there is liberty," (2 Corinthians 3:17). Real freedom is where the Spirit of the Lord is present. Holy Spirit is the Spirit of the Lord, and not just your friend or teacher. If Jesus is not your Lord, then Holy Spirit's power is limited in your life. His power is only unleashed and brings freedom in our lives when Jesus is truly our Lord. I heard someone explain once that this verse can also be read as, "Where the Spirit is Lord, there is freedom."

Surrendering to the Lordship of Jesus changes how we think, speak, live, spend our money, and treat other people—but it also changes how the Devil sees us.

When Japan attacked Pearl Harbor in 1941, the United States of America went to war against Japan. In 1945 Japan signed a complete and unconditional surrender to the Allied Forces. The United States, who had retaliated against Japan, now led an economic recovery plan. Japan recovered from the destructions of Hiroshima and Nagasaki; and now it is one of the most productive and peaceful countries in the world. Japan does not have a military; the USA is their covering. The United States took full responsibility for the recovery and protection of the nation that surrendered to them. If we want God to have our back and have his full protection, we must fully surrender to Him.

Some people do not want Jesus as their King, and only want Him as a good teacher. In this life, there is no middle ground, we are either God's servants or the Devil's slaves. Yes, we are God's children, but in our hearts, we must never digress from a place of surrender, to a place of selfishness.

If we truly have Jesus as our Lord, He will guide us and use us for His kingdom. But if we are our own lords, we will use Jesus for our own selfish purposes.

Confront the Enemy

There are many people who receive freedom when someone prays for them. Either by someone with an anointing, or from a ministry that ministers to those in captivity and are in need of deliverance. It is wise to seek prayer from a pastor or a deliverance minister.

God gave different gifts and levels of anointing to different people, but we also have a role to play. God's Spirit lives in us and He desires to bring freedom into our lives. No matter who prays for us, or does not pray for us, it is Jesus and Holy Spirit's power that brings about change.

David was delivered from a lion and a bear. He recalls how God delivered him when he testified before King Saul, "When a lion or a bear came and took a lamb out of the flock, I went out after it and struck it, and delivered the lamb from its mouth; and when it arose against me, I caught it by its beard, and struck and killed it. Your servant has killed both lion and bear," (1 Samuel 17:34-36).

David did not run from the lion or the bear, he went after them and fought with them. Moreover, David said, "The Lord, who delivered me from the paw of the lion and from the paw of the bear, He will deliver me from the hand of this Philistine," (1 Samuel 17:37). God delivered David from the lion and the bear when he went after them, not when he ran from them. Could it be the same way, that God brings deliverance to those who do not play the victim? Yes, these types of believers do not hope for someone to pray for them, but instead, claim their place in Jesus' authority, confront the enemy, and secure victory for their life! Do not hide, instead, fight. In the Bible, James says to submit to God and resist the Devil. We have a role to play in our freedom by submitting and resisting.

Confronting the enemy begins with renouncing every vow, oath, ritual, blood covenant, sorcery, witchcraft, divination, false religion, doctrine of demons, false worship, and all kind of curses. When we renounce those things, it cuts the chain connected to us. "But we have renounced the hidden things of shame, not walking in craftiness nor handling the word of God deceitfully, but by manifestation of the truth commending ourselves to every man's conscience in the sight of God," (2 Corinthians 4:2). To see the manifestation of truth, to handle God's word truthfully, and to walk in honesty, we must first renounce the hidden things of shame and sins that have opened the door to darkness.

Resist the Enemy

Recognizing our need for freedom, repenting from sin, and renouncing all connection with the Devil will get us out of the Egyptian slavery. This begins the process of getting Egypt out of us. This takes place by resisting the Devil, replacing our habits, and renewing our minds.

God supernaturally delivered Israel from Egypt by the blood of the lamb, which is a foreshadow of the cross of Jesus Christ. They came out of the house of bondage rejoicing. Joy is the natural response when receiving long awaited freedom. This joy was cut short a few days later when chariots of the army of Egypt came to take Israel back into bondage. Egypt had lost its workers, which meant all their construction projects came to a halt. Pharaoh and his army came with the intention of defeating freed people, and putting them back into their old lifestyle. Israel's response — as they always did — was panic, fear, and lots of complaining.

If God set us free, why is Pharaoh pursuing us? Are we really free if the Egyptians are not completely gone? It is pretty normal — even after experiencing deliverance — to still have the same attacks of the enemy as one had prior to deliverance. This experience will cause a person to question their freedom. The Devil's goal — through confusion and doubt — is to bring a person back into a place of bondage in their mind and life. When our old demons come back with their chariots, after we have been set free, it does not necessarily mean we are back in bondage. Many times, God is trying to set you free and bring permanent freedom to your life by, once and for all, drowning that Pharaoh in the sea.

It is confirmed by Jesus that when a demon leaves a person, it will seek to come back with more demons (see Matthew 12:45). This should not scare us. Pharaoh came back with chariots, but Israel did not end up going back into slavery, because they went forward in faith and obedience. The Devil will try, through doubt and lies, to get back into your soul, but you should not change your position and confession by yielding to his lies.

We must resist him by standing in faith (see 1 Peter 5:9). We must believe that we are free after we repent and renounce all demonic connection. This attack is not a sign that you are not free. Instead, it is the Devil's last attempt to take you back into bondage. We must learn to walk forward in faith. God will drown Pharaoh, and our freedom will be true freedom, secure and permanent. The Devil cannot get us back into bondage if we are moving forward in faith. Even if we fall into the same sin that we have been delivered from, we must repent and receive forgiveness, forgive ourselves, get up, and march forward as though it never happened.

Getting freed does not mean we will never again be under attack. Similarly, when we got saved, it did not mean we would never sin again. The righteous man falls seven times and gets back up (see Proverbs 24:16). In other words, we do not stop being righteous because we fall. The only time we stop being righteous is when we choose to live in what we fell into. We are a righteous and freed people now — we should hate sin when we happen to fall into it. This is a sign that it is not our identity anymore. When a sheep falls into the mud, it then begins to cry. When a pig falls into the mud, it plays in it. We are sheep, and not pigs, when we fall.

One of the guys at our church was delivered from the spirit of pornography. His deliverance was powerful. He was sure he was freed and for the next two months, he did not struggle with lust. After a two-month period, he fell back into that sin. He asked to meet with me, so I knew something was wrong. When he confessed what happened, he shared how he was confused, because he felt he was no longer free. The deliverance he received was in Nigeria. He wanted to know if he should save his money to go back to Nigeria and receive deliverance once again. I told him, "Whether you believe you are delivered, or whether you believe you are not delivered, you are right." My suggestion to him was to choose to believe that he is still delivered. He had to stand on that truth, and continue to walk in freedom as if it never happened. After that incident, permanent freedom came to this young man, who also happens to be one of our powerful leaders, and is now a married man.

We must go forward in faith if we want our freedom to become our lifestyle. We cannot let the Devil drag us backwards in fear, doubt, or confusion. In the upcoming chapters we will discuss this in more detail—the principle of changing and renewing the mind. The next chapter talks about one of the biggest keys to freedom.

Prayer

"*You Devil, behind my addiction; and you demon, behind repeated sin and failure—I do not come against you in my name, but in the name of my Lord and Savior, Jesus Christ. I, now, command you to leave my life. I, now, break your grip over my mind, emotions, and my will. Every chain that Satan might have used to connect himself to me, is broken, now, in Jesus' name. Anything not planted by my Father, in my life, is to be uprooted in Jesus' name, right now! I stand in Jesus' authority and in the power of the Spirit of God, and I resist the Devil with all his thoughts of doubt, fear, and condemnation. I put up a shield of faith against his flaming arrows of lies.*"

CHAPTER 7

THE BAIT OF SATAN

I heard a powerful testimony on the Sid Roth show, "It's Supernatural," about this guy named Frank. He had a very rough life. As a child he was sexually molested which later developed into unresolved hurt and rebellion. Frank signed up for the Naval Academy, but got kicked out, because of using and selling drugs. After that he started to hear voices that would lead him into good luck. These voices would tell him where to hide his drugs to avoid getting caught. Life seemed great, doing drugs, and getting protection from listening to voices. One of these voices also led him to draw a pentagram, which is a demonic symbol, and afterward, a spirit entered Frank.

No longer were voices guiding him, now he was being tormented. Through drugs, demons drew a new reality in his mind that the world had been invaded, he was the only one left, and he needed to stay alive to avoid being captured by aliens. A voice would tell him that everyone he saw was there to capture and infect him, and he must destroy them. So, he did just that. He took a hammer and started attacking people, putting eight individuals into the hospital. One received permanent brain damage, and two were murdered. All of this occurred while he was being led by a voice saying that this world was being invaded by another world.

When the police arrested him, they said that he exhibited supernatural strength, seven to eight times more than a normal human being. When Frank was in the hospital, he thought that he was captured by aliens, so he decided to commit suicide. He took a jar and slammed it onto himself, hoping to bleed to death. The staff stopped the bleeding in time. He was sentenced to 10-30 years in prison, because the murders were not premeditated. While in jail, he came off the drugs and the voices subsided. He finally realized he was deceived by the Devil.

The widow of one of the men murdered by him came to visit him. He was not sure why she wanted to meet him. Upon meeting him, she offered him forgiveness for murdering her husband. She believed that God works out all things for good, and the only way something good could come out of this tragedy, would be if Frank would accept Jesus Christ—then the death of her husband would not have been in vain. The widow gave her husband's Bible to the killer. He decided to read it to honor the widow's request.

In the process of this, he accepted Jesus Christ and received deliverance from the demonic spirit. God even gave him a wife— one of the women who came to prison to do jail ministry. He was a restored man. After 13 years of sitting in jail, he was finally released from prison and went to the widow's church to share his testimony of how forgiveness can change a murderer into an evangelist, and the dangers of playing games with the Devil.

Today, his ministry has led many hard-core murderers, rapists, prisoners, and crazy people to grow in relationship with Jesus. Forgiveness brings freedom.

Skandalon

The most commonly used Greek word for an offense— Skandalon—is stated in the New Testament in Matthew 18:7. Skandalon is the trigger of a trap, on which bait is placed. When an animal touches the trigger to eat the bait, the trap springs shut and the animal is caught. An offense is an enticement to a conduct which will ruin the person in question.

When my wife and I lived in a duplex, I saw that in the basement we had a mouse. I cannot stand those little creatures, and the knowledge that they were running around when I slept, gave me the chills. I knew that I was not fast enough to catch them with my hands or kill them with a stick. I did what every good homeowner would do. I got into my car, drove to Wal-Mart, and bought some mouse traps. I put bacon and peanut butter as bait on the trap, and I left the trap to work its magic. I would never be able to get rid of the mouse if the mouse would resist the urge to eat bacon and peanut butter. I never forced it to get to the bait. In fact, I was not present in the house when the mouse got its back snapped by the force of the trigger. That is exactly how the Devil works.

You see, he cannot get to us directly, because we are covered by the blood, serving God, and walking in the Spirit. We are annoying to him, because we disturb his kingdom and ruin his plans on earth. So, the Devil has been using an indirect method to get to us — the best method, since the beginning of creation — offense.

Jesus teaches us that we are unable to avoid encountering offenses (see Luke 17:1). As long as there are people on earth, there will be pain and hurt. Even if you live holy before the Holy God, you will get hurt. Abel did, Joseph did, David did, Jesus did, and so will you.

The only thing we can do is avoid causing offenses to others (see 1 Corinthians 8:13), but we cannot avoid bad things from happening to us. When we get hurt, the Devil wants to use anger, grudges, bitterness, and resentment to make us feel like we are in control. No one can hurt us again, because we build walls around us to keep people away. It is a trap, the Devil's bait.

Wounds Neglected Become Infected

Wounds speak of hurt, scars speak of healing. A wound says, "Look at what they did." A scar says, "Look how God healed me." Wounds hurt, scars do not. Wounds lead to infection, scars lead to testimony. Our Savior was wounded for our transgressions (see Isaiah 53:5). When He was hanging on the cross, He did not threaten the Pharisees or curse them while being in agony. He forgave them. They did not deserve it; they did not even ask for it. Frankly, they did not think that what they were doing was wrong. Jesus did not forgive them so that their sin would be forgiven, but so His own heart would not turn to bitterness.

As I mentioned before, betrayal is what people do to you, bitterness is what you do to you. Betrayal is external, bitterness is internal. The only thing that turns betrayal into blessing is forgiveness.

Jesus did not stay on the cross forever. People can put you on the cross, but only unforgiveness keeps you there. Your enemies can put you in a painful pit, but only unforgiveness keeps you there. We must understand that the first time this incident happens to us, we are victims. The second time, we relive it in our minds as volunteers. Yes, we volunteer for this by our offense and unforgiveness.

Forgiveness on the cross protected Jesus' heart, and modeled to us how to handle our most painful situations. A few days after the resurrection, Jesus came to His disciples without wounds, only scars. He asked them to touch those scars. You still have wounds if you cannot talk about the painful parts of your past without pain. Jesus' scars brought hope and healing to His disciples' faith.

If you let God turn your wounds into scars, He will turn your scars into testimonies. He will redeem what the Devil meant for evil. If you do not have scars, it is not because you have not been hurt. Instead, it is most likely due to your not being healed. Even Jesus had scars.

Escaping the Torture Chamber

Unforgiveness is the legal right of the Devil to your heart. Matthew documents a parable by Jesus on how unforgiveness puts us into the hands of torturers (see Matthew 18:34). Torturers are demons who torment people who refuse to forgive. These demons do not leave when you rebuke them, they only exit when you forgive.

We must forgive because God needs it. If we do not forgive, God does not forgive us (see Matthew 6:15).

We must forgive because we need it. Forgiveness does not change the past, rather it enlarges the future. When you forgive, you set the prisoner free and then you discover that the prisoner was you. If you wait for those who hurt you to ask for forgiveness, that day may never come. Forgive them for your sake, not theirs. Forgiveness is a decision of the will. It is when you release that person from owing you anything. You surrender your right to hurt them for hurting you when you speak a blessing over them. Feelings of revenge and hurt will surface again and again, but you have to go back to the initial decision that you made to forgive them. Do not let those feelings convince you that you did not forgive, instead, replace those feelings by speaking a blessing over that person and yourself.

I heard a testimony about Frida, a survivor of the Rwandan Genocide. She witnessed her family being massacred with machetes by the Hutu men, and was then asked how she wanted to die. Because they did not have any more bullets, they buried her alive along with her slaughtered family. Fourteen hours later, some relatives came looking for the family members to give them a proper burial. They found that the little girl was still alive and conscious. Because of that trauma, she had headaches, problems with her back, and constant nightmares. At one seminar she heard about the power of forgiveness. The moment she forgave, God instantly healed and delivered her from nightmares.

Today she is a spokeswoman and an author of the book, "Frida: Chosen to Die, Destined to Live," carrying a powerful message about the power of forgiveness and love for our enemies.[10]

When we forgive, we not only get freed, but we give God an opportunity to redeem our pain for our purpose.

The Hardest Person to Forgive

The hardest person to forgive is not always your enemy, it is actually yourself. Many people are hurting today, even after God forgave them, because they, in return, did not forgive themselves. John Stott, administrator of the largest psychiatric hospital in London, said, "If people here only knew what it means to be forgiven, I could dismiss half of them at once." You must receive the gift of forgiveness from God and give it to yourself if you want to live in freedom. It is not easy to do it at times. Instead of forgiving ourselves as Christ forgave us, we punish ourselves in hopes that it will show to God that we really understand the severity of our actions. Whatever the reason is for self-punishment for our sins, we must understand that, at its root, lies distrust in the Gospel.

The guilt and shame of betrayal led Judas to hang himself. Not very far from him, Jesus was hanged on the cross for everyone's sin, including Judas'. You do not need to punish yourself. Your sin was already punished. Of the last sayings of Christ on the cross, none is more important or poignant than, "It is finished." Found only in the Gospel of John, the Greek wording, "It is finished," is translated as "tetelestai," an accounting term meaning, "paid in full." When

Jesus uttered those words, He declared that the debt owed to His Father was wiped away completely and forever. Not that Jesus wiped away any debt that He owed to the Father; rather, Jesus eliminated the debt owed by mankind—the debt of sin. His payment was enough, you do not need to add anything to it. Your suffering is not needed for your forgiveness to be complete.

When you confess your sin, God is true and just to forgive your sins (see 1 John 1:9). If God, Who is holy, can forgive you, a sinner, then you, as a sinner, can forgive a sinner as yourself. When you do not forgive yourself, you are telling God that your standards are higher than His. In fact, you are telling God that you are tougher on your sin than He is. It takes humility to look at God's forgiveness toward us and gift that to ourselves. To forgive yourself, you must receive it from God first.

Asking God for forgiveness is good, receiving that forgiveness is where the breakthrough lies. I often meet people who keep asking God to forgive them for a particular sin. He forgave them when they asked the first time. They simply failed to receive it by faith.

There was a priest in the Philippines, who in his youth, committed a horrible sin for which he could not forgive himself. Constantly, he would ask God to forgive him again and again for that act. Now, he had his own parish, yet the struggled to forgive himself plagued his spiritual walk with God. One day a lady came to confess, and instead of confessing her sin, she told the priest that Jesus visited her. He told the lady to stop making up stories and coming to share fairy tales. She kept coming back to the confession booth sharing how Jesus visited her all of the time. So finally, the priest decided to put her to the test. He asked her to ask Jesus to tell her what he did in college. He said to himself, if she will tell him what he did, then maybe Jesus does appear to her after all. Now this sin was on his mind all the time, it must mean that it was on Jesus' mind as well.

The next day the lady came to her confession with excitement, which made the priest a little bit nervous. She said, "Father, Jesus came yesterday."

"What did he say about what happened while I was at college," the priest queried?

The woman replied, "Jesus said that He forgave you and forgot about it, and you should as well." The priest learned a powerful lesson to forgive himself, because God forgave him.

"As far as the east is from the west, so far has He removed our transgressions from us," (Psalm 103:12). God removed your sin from you. He dropped them in the sea of forgetfulness and put a sign there saying, "No fishing." "I, even I, am He who blots out your transgressions for My own sake; and I will not remember your sins," (Isaiah 43:25). God blots out our sin and chooses to not remember them again. If He did that when we sinned against Him, we should do the same to ourselves, forgive and forget.

By forgetting, I mean we choose not to dwell on it and punish ourselves for it. God, in Christ, has forgiven you, now receive that by faith. Forgive yourself; it will free you from repeating that sin again. Guilt and shame promise to help us stay away from that sin, but they fail to deliver on their promise. Only grace keeps us from sin. Grace is found in forgiveness.

Don't Charge God with Wrong

Receiving forgiveness, and giving forgiveness to others and yourself, are keys to freedom, but some people also need to forgive God. Not in the sense that God sinned against them, but in the sense that they hold God hostage to something He did not do, but was supposed to have done. Satan seeks to create an offense towards God, so that he drives us away from Him. At a certain point in your life, the Devil will set a bait for you to question God. Why did God allow the death of a loved one? Why did He not heal someone we prayed for? Why did God not stop an accident from taking place? Why did He not protect us from heart break?

The idea that if God is with us then nothing bad will ever happen to us, is not from Scripture. God's presence does not mean there will not be unfair things happening around us. God was with Joseph, yet he was rejected, betrayed, sold, falsely accused, imprisoned, and forgotten. God was with the Hebrew boys, Shadrach, Meshach, and Abednego, yet they were rejected and thrown into the fire to be killed. God was with Jesus, yet He was rejected, misunderstood, physically beaten, forsaken, and crucified.

In all of our trials and tribulations, we must never blame God or allow the Devil to make our heart hard toward the Lord. It is a trap. When hell broke loose in Job's life, he grieved and worshipped. "In all this Job did not sin nor charge God with wrong," (Job 1:22). If you felt like God let you down, was not there for you, and you hold God hostage or charge Him with wrong, you have to repent and release those feelings. Blaming God for the bad in this world is like blaming the Secretary of Transportation for the accidents on the road. It is not fair. We live in a broken world where men choose darkness. Everyone's decisions affect those around them. God, in the midst of all this mess, chooses to be with us and lead us out of affliction for a greater purpose.

I always tell young people, "If God fails to meet your expectations, trust Him to exceed them." If you do not let offense build in your heart towards God, He will show you His glory.

Jesus had friends, Mary and Martha. One day, their brother, Lazarus, got sick and died. Jesus did not come in time to heal Lazarus. Mary and Martha were disappointed. If we would have been in their place, we would've been disappointed as well. It seemed like Jesus made time for everyone else, but His friends. Jesus finally came when Lazarus was long gone. They were asking for a miracle, but Jesus planned a resurrection.

Sometimes your expectations will be ruined, so that God can do something greater than you ever imagined. Do not get stuck in your disappointment. When things get hard, do not let this ruin your heart's response to God.

When Things Go from Bad to Worse

Jesus makes our life better and makes us better at life. This is generally true. He came to give us life and more abundantly (see John 10:10). On our way to that abundant life, we might experience unexpected delays, disappointments, and discouragement. When the leader of the Synagogue had a sick daughter, he knew where to go for help. He went to Jesus, and Jesus agreed to help. On the way to the house, the daughter's condition worsened and she died. People who brought this news to the father told him to leave Jesus alone now. Sometimes, walking with Jesus makes things go from bad to worse. What do we do when this happens? Blame Jesus? Leave Jesus? Or keep on walking with Him? Jesus told the man who just heard the worst news possible, "Don't be afraid, only believe," (see Mark 5:36). Jesus then raised that little girl from the dead.

The lesson is this, when things go from bad to worse, do not stop doing what you were doing with God, instead, keep on going. Building an offense in your heart, or thinking that you were better off when you were serving the Devil, should not be an option.

I would rather go through hell on my way to heaven, than go through heaven on my way to hell.

When things go from bad to worse, turn your worse into worship, and then God will turn your worship into wonders.

Prayer

"Dear Lord, I have benefited from the gift of Your forgiveness to me, and I choose to forgive those who have hurt me. Help me set [name anyone who has offended you] free and release them to You. I bless those who hurt me. Help them walk in righteousness, peace, and joy. Lord Jesus, today, I also ask forgiveness for the all negative and harmful feelings I have held against myself. I do not want to abuse myself in such a way. I forgive myself for things I have done, as You have forgiven me. Any offense that I have toward You, today, for my failed expectations, I let that go. I refuse to charge You, God, with wrong. I choose to worship and trust in Your unfailing love. Help me Holy Spirit."

CHAPTER 8

REAL FREEDOM

Brian grew up in a broken home where his parents got divorced when he was only six years of age. His family would go camping every weekend, where alcohol was the order of the day. At a tender age, it became normal for him to see so much drinking. By the age of 14, he began to do exactly the same thing his family had showed him. Drinking then led him to taking opioid painkillers, which eventually became an addiction. Then, towards the end of his high school years, he began to smoke weed.

After graduation, his opioid addiction led to heroin use. He was kicked out of his home, lost his job, and was living on the streets with other people similar to himself, whose only purpose was to get high. Once, while driving with his girlfriend, they were pulled over and his girlfriend was arrested. The car was impounded and he had to walk to his mom's house. On the way to his mom's, he fell to the ground, unconscious, because of the drug use. A short time afterwards, he was found by his mom, laying on the street. This addiction had a strong grip on his life and led him to overdose several more times. Then one day, at a friend's apartment, he stopped breathing, so they had to put him in the shower to bring him back to consciousness. Later on, he would overdose four more times over the period of one and a half months. During one of those times, he was actually declared dead at the scene, but miraculously recovered. However, none of these incidents were enough to spark a desire for freedom.

Soon after, his girlfriend brought news to him—she was pregnant and he was going to be a father. The news shocked him so much that he decided to admit himself for professional help. After being released from rehab he found out that it was not his kid, but someone else was the father. His freedom from drugs was motivated by a lie. However, he followed through with drug court, by going to all AA and NA meetings, and admitted himself into an Oxford house.

At that time, my sister invited him via Facebook to our service. People talked about God at the Oxford house, but Brian did not want anything to do with it. He did not grow up in a religious home, so God was a foreign topic to him. He chose to honor my sister's request and came to church. Later he shared in his testimony, how church felt awkward for him. The whole concept of God was weird to him; people praying out loud, speaking in tongues, and the atmosphere was uncomfortable—but he came again. My cousin, Nazar, decided to pick him up for every service, and also brought him to his homegroup. Brian said that if it had not been for Nazar checking in on him, calling, and meeting with him, he would not have come back over and over again.

After a few months, Brian gave his life to Jesus and got water baptized. He started to get involved in the church and was coming to our 5 a.m. morning prayers. He also finished our summer internship program. His homegroup leader, Nazar, blessed him with a very nice car. Brian's life was turning around towards God's new direction. I recall attending his legal testimony in court, when all his charges were dropped. He bravely shared about Christ and the power of God, that brought about positive change in his life. That day happened to be a Wednesday, and his mom, who lived in a different state, surprised him by visiting his court hearing. That evening, at the church service, his mom also gave her life to Jesus. Both of them are now part of our local church. Brian later became a group leader to other guys.

Today, Brian is overseeing our ushers team and working towards his Bachelor's degree in business. Jesus wants to set us free and give us a purpose for our lives. Freedom is not just so we can do what we want, but to do what God wants us to do.

Loosen that Donkey and Bring it to Me

There is a beautiful analogy of the purpose for freedom, from the story about the donkey in Matthew 21:1-11. The donkey had received a prophecy long before it was born. It is just like you. God had a plan for your life before you were born. You are not an accident. You came from God, but through your parents. God thought of you before you were even conceived. Though the donkey had a prophecy about its life, we see that the donkey was bound at the time Jesus wanted to use it for His purpose.

A lot of times the Devil will bind you before God can use you. The reason is that you will be restricted from following God's call. The chains of addiction, low self-esteem, abuse, fear, and condemnation have one assignment, which is to hold you back from what you were created for. Jesus sent His two disciples to find and loose the donkey. When Israel was under Egypt's bondage, God sent Moses. When Israel was in bondage to the Philistines, God sent Samson, Samuel, Saul, and David. When you are in bondage to sin, God has already sent His Son, Jesus Christ, to set you free.

You are loosed from your chains, so that you can be used in your calling. Jesus told His disciples to loosen that donkey and bring it to Him. The disciples were not instructed to set the donkey free and let it go where it wanted to go. Freedom was with a purpose. Freedom was on purpose. The purpose of the freedom was not to do what the donkey wanted to do, but to do what Jesus wanted to do with the donkey. The donkey was not fully free when its chains were removed, but when Jesus sat on it. Real freedom is not removal of sin, it is when Jesus replaces that sin by being the center of your life where your sin used to be. There is purpose for your freedom. If you think your freedom is so that you can do what you want, then you become an easy target for the Devil.

After you are freed, you are either a vehicle for God's will on earth, or an easy target for your enemy. The donkey was most free, not when the ropes were removed from its neck, but when Jesus sat on its back. The amount of control sin has over you, is the amount of bondage you have. The amount of control Jesus has over you, is how much freedom you have. You are free when demons are gone and your chains are broken, but it is only the beginning. Real and lasting freedom is when God takes the place of sin that Satan used to occupy. This steers you to become even more loyal to God than you were to the Devil.

When Jesus sat on the donkey, the donkey gave Jesus a ride to the city and the city was moved. When Jesus is the Lord of your life, He will use you. When you are the lord of your life, you will use God for selfish reasons. The real purpose of your freedom, is to give Jesus full control of your life and bring Jesus into your city, school, and workplace. Let your generation be moved by the Jesus you carry. That is the reason freedom was given to the donkey, and the same goes for you.

That They Might Serve Me

The exodus from Egypt is another great illustration of what it is like to be set free from the bondage of sin and Satan. Why did God deliver Israel out of their bondage? Was it because He made a promise to Abraham to deliver them? Was it because God is a just God, and Egypt treated Israel unjustly? Was it because Israel had a promised land to possess? While it is true that God brought the exodus because of His promise to Abraham, and broke the injustice done to Israel and helped them conquer their inheritance, the real motive behind the exodus is revealed in the following verses:

"The Lord God of the Hebrews has met with us; and now, please, let us go three days' journey into the wilderness, *that we may sacrifice to the Lord our God,"* (Exodus 3:18).

"Let My people go, that they may hold a feast to Me in the wilderness," (Exodus 5:1).

"The God of the Hebrews has met with us. Please, let us go three days' journey into the desert and *sacrifice to the Lord our God,* lest He fall upon us with pestilence or with the sword," (Exodus 5:3).

"And you shall lay on them the quota of bricks which they made before. You shall not reduce it. For they are idle; therefore, they cry out, saying, '*Let us go and sacrifice to our God,'*" (Exodus 5:8).

"And you shall say to him, 'The Lord God of the Hebrews has sent me to you, saying, "Let My people go, *that they may serve Me in the wilderness*"; but indeed, until now you would not hear!'" (Exodus 7:16).

"And the Lord spoke to Moses, 'Go to Pharaoh and say to him, "Thus says the Lord: 'Let My people go, *that they may serve Me,'*"'" (Exodus 8:1).

"Then Pharaoh called for Moses and Aaron, and said, 'Entreat the Lord that He may take away the frogs from me and from my people; and I will let the people go, *that they may sacrifice to the Lord,'*" (Exodus 8:8).

"And the Lord said to Moses, 'Rise early in the morning and stand before Pharaoh as he comes out to the water. Then say to him, "Thus says the Lord: 'Let My people go, *that they may serve Me,'*"'" (Exodus 8:20).

"Then Pharaoh called for Moses and Aaron, and said, 'Go, *sacrifice to your God in the land*,'" (Exodus 8:25).

"So, Pharaoh said, 'I will let you go, *that you may sacrifice to the Lord your God in the wilderness*; only you shall not go very far away. Intercede for me.'" (Exodus 8:28).

"Then the Lord said to Moses, 'Go in to Pharaoh and tell him, "Thus says the Lord God of the Hebrews: 'Let My people go, *that they may serve Me*,'"'" (Exodus 9:1).

"Then the Lord said to Moses, 'Rise early in the morning and stand before Pharaoh, and say to him, "Thus says the Lord God of the Hebrews: 'Let My people go, *that they may serve Me*,'"'" (Exodus 9:13).

"So, Moses and Aaron came in to Pharaoh and said to him, 'Thus says the Lord God of the Hebrews: "How long will you refuse to humble yourself before Me? Let My people go, *that they may serve Me*,"'" (Exodus 10:3).

"Then Pharaoh's servants said to him, 'How long shall this man be a snare to us? Let the men go, *that they may serve the Lord their God*. Do you not yet know that Egypt is destroyed?'" (Exodus 10:7).

"Then Pharaoh called to Moses and said, 'Go, *serve the Lord*; only let your flocks and your herds be kept back. Let your little ones also go with you,'" (Exodus 10:24).

"Then he called for Moses and Aaron by night, and said, 'Rise, go out from among my people, both you and the children of Israel. And go, *serve the Lord as you have said*,'" (Exodus 12:31).

It is pretty clear that God was setting Israel free from Egypt so they would be free to serve Him. This was not a lie, nor an excuse Moses used when speaking to Pharaoh to make it easier for the Egyptians to let Israel go. Serving and sacrificing to God was the main reason God showed His power in bringing powerful deliverance from their enemy.

The promised land was the goal, but serving God was the reason for the exodus. God knew that Israel couldn't serve Him fully as long as they were Pharaoh's slaves. As long as we are on the payroll of sin, we cannot be fully available to Jesus. Sadly, just like Israel, we do not see freedom for that reason. We want to be free, so that we do not have to live in shame, guilt, poverty, and hurting others; so that perhaps we do not have to go to hell. Israel thought that freedom was about them being relieved from hardships of injustice.

God was not interested in only removing the enemy, He was interested in replacing the enemy with Himself. He wanted to be the Master of them, instead of the monster, Pharaoh, that they had. He wanted them to serve Him as sons, for they had served the evil Pharaoh as slaves.

The Israelites were better slaves to Pharaoh than they were servants to God. Many people were better servants to their addiction and past lives of sin, than they are to God and His purpose for them as His children. The exodus was not to give them a better life primarily, but to provide them with a better Master. God was to replace Pharaoh. They liked the idea of God being their Deliverer, but submitting to Him as their Lord did not come easy for many of the freed slaves. Are you as good (if not even better) of a servant to God as you were a slave to the Devil?

Definition of Freedom

We define freedom as the removal of something evil, but Apostle Paul saw freedom differently. "And where the Spirit of the Lord is, there is liberty," (2 Corinthians 3:17). There is freedom where the Spirit is present. Paul did not say freedom is when the chains are gone, curses broken, and demons cast out. When someone no longer has an addiction, is that when they are free? When a demon is expelled is that when freedom comes? If the Spirit of God did not take the place where sin and addiction used to occupy, that person is not yet free.

Freedom is not just removal of evil, but the presence of God's Spirit. When you are freed from Satan, only to be filled with your own desires, it is bondage, not freedom. So many people get free, only so they can live their life to the fullest. That is dangerous. That is wrong. Jesus did not set you free so that you can, now, erect yourself as the god of your life. Your sins were removed by the mighty blood of Jesus, so that you can serve God at least to the capacity that you used to serve the Devil.

If you make your life about yourself after freedom, or if you look forward to freedom so you can do what you want, that is not full freedom. If you switch rooms, or pods, in a jail building, you are still in jail even if you are on a different floor. Going into selfishness after being set free from Satan is still bondage.

Freedom is not doing what you want, it is doing what you ought—being available to do what God wants. Satanism is based on one big idea, "do what thou wilt", meaning, "do what you want." Satanism is not just about worshipping Satan, it is worshipping your own self. When we get rid of addiction, demons, and curses, only to worship self, we are still in bondage.

Move From "Give Me" to "Make Me"

When we are born again, we become children of God. That is our identity, our position in Christ. As sons we must possess the heart of serving. Jesus was the Son of God, yet He was obedient through His death on the cross, following the will of the Father. He came to serve and die for God's purpose. Unfortunately, many people today think that being a son gives them self-entitlement, they no longer need to die to their selfishness. They use God to get what they want, instead of letting God use them to accomplish His will.

Satan tempted Jesus in the wilderness, and on the cross, with this idea – if you are the Son of God, you do not need to serve, nor give your life to fulfill God's will. Jesus rejected that notion. Sadly, many Christians have bought into this lie that, "I am a son, I do not need to serve." When we only stand in the position of a son, but have no heart of a servant, we are no better than the prodigal son.

The prodigal son knew his rights, but did not have a clue about his responsibly in the house. He was a great son, but a terrible servant. He did not hate his father, he just loved himself. The prodigal son did not go against his father, he went away from him. All of his prayers were summed up in this "give me what is mine." At first, this seems like a good thing to ask, but he had no desire to be with his father, or to do his will. He was there to use his father to get what he wanted. He got what he wanted, but he did not want what he got.

His sonship did not protect him from living with pigs because his heart was not the heart of a servant. He learned his lesson while being with the pigs. When he came back to his father, he no longer asked for things, but for the father to make him like one of his servants. He always had been a son, but only now, he realized he needed to learn to be a servant.

You were born as a son, but you must develop a servant spirit, otherwise your freedom will be lost to the bondage of selfishness. Selfishness is one step away from living life with the swine. When you become a believer, you are a son or daughter. When you become a disciple, you are a servant. Sonship is free, discipleship costs everything. It costs your ego and pride. If it cost Jesus His entire life, it will cost you no less.

There are only three things you can do with your life, wreck it by living in sin, waste it by living in selfishness, or lay it down as a sacrifice to the Savior. Freedom is transferring from sin and selfishness, so that you can lay your life down as a living sacrifice to the One who died for you.

Prayer

"Father God, I search my heart, today, and examine my motives in the light of Your Word. I acknowledge that I want to be free, so that I do not live in the pain of bondage, but my real desire is to do what I want to do, without any hindrance from the Devil. I am sorry for that. I want what You want for the same reasons You want it. I know that You want all of me. So, I ask along with the prodigal son, make me Your servant, be my Lord. I refuse to use You as a means to reach my goals. You are my goal, You are my exceedingly great reward."

CHAPTER 9

BREAKING STRONGHOLDS

Scientists did a study on barracuda fish, which are larger fish that eat other smaller fish. They put barracuda fish into a fish tank and dropped smaller fish in there as well. The barracuda fish attacked them. After that, they put a glass in the middle of the tank. A barracuda fish was put on one side of the tank and smaller fish were put on the other side of the tank. The glass barrier was invisible, so the barracuda fish went to attack the other smaller fish head on, and hit the glass hard. It kept hitting the glass at first, then it began to slowly approach the glass to touch it. After a few days, the glass was removed, and surprisingly the barracuda fish never swam to the other side to attack the smaller fish. They came to the conclusion that even though the glass barrier was removed from the tank, it was still engraved in the mind of the fish.

We all hit certain glass walls in our lives, and after repeated failures, these defeats enter us. Even if these limits would be removed in the spiritual realm, we would still be limited, because it also needs to be removed in our minds.

The Strongman Lives in a Stronghold

Jesus said, "Or how can one enter a strong man's house and plunder his goods, unless he first binds the strong man?" (Matthew 12:29). The strong man is an evil spirit that plunders a person's peace, joy, finances, and health. We must bind the strong man in order to get freedom from him. The strongman is a demon, a stronghold is a house of thoughts. "For the weapons of our warfare

are not carnal but mighty in God for pulling down strongholds," (2 Corinthians 10:4). Our weapons are powerful for binding the strongman and for breaking down strongholds.

We must understand that demons come quickly and usually exit at the same speed. Strongholds are built over time and get destroyed over time. The Devil is not only interested in breaking your life, but also building a mindset in you, so that even when he is gone, you will still live in pain as though he is still there. A stronghold is the house the Devil builds in your mind. It is a house for the strongman.

This house of thoughts includes repeated thoughts of doubt, fear, condemnation, unworthiness, lies, and negativity. It takes the Devil a while to build this in our minds, but once it is built, he has a place to call home. Strongholds are the Devil's residence. You can expel demons, but if you do not break down the strongholds, he can still torment your life by the mindset he formed in you.

A Stronghold is a Mindset

There was an experiment done with a millionaire and a homeless person. The millionaire was put in a homeless situation, and the homeless person received one million dollars. The experimenters wanted to monitor their behavior to see if money fixed the homeless man's problem. Within a short period of time the person who was initially a millionaire, but was made homeless, got an idea for a new business. He was not allowed to reach out to his old contacts, or do a business he was accustomed to doing. Not long afterward, his new business went into full bloom, and he became a millionaire again from scratch. The homeless person wasted most of the money he was given by living a wasteful life, and ended up back on the streets again. Those in charge of the experiment came to the conclusion that being a millionaire is more about your mindset than about your money.

A mindset, or stronghold, is very powerful. Our mind is what we can control, but our mindset controls us. Most of our behaviors are automatic. Our subconscious mind is much more powerful than our conscious mind. Our mindset becomes the magnet for things. For example, if you are filled with constant negative thoughts, they, in return, attract more negative things into your life. That is why Jesus said, "For to everyone who has, more will be given, and he will have abundance; but from him who does not have, even what he has will be taken away," (Matthew 25:29). Whatever your mind is filled with, it will naturally draw the same substance until your life is overflowing with a reality of your most dominant thoughts. Some people's failure in life is not demonic, but mental. Mental strongholds can only be broken by the truth of God's Word.

Touch and Teach

When Jesus addressed the issue of freedom in the Gospel of John, chapter 8, He said, 'Whom the Son sets free is free indeed.' This deals with casting out demons and breaking generational curses. When Jesus drives out evil spirits by His touch, they are expelled. In the same place, Jesus also made a reference that if we know the truth, the truth will set us free. The question that arises is if we receive all freedom from Jesus by His setting us free, why do we still need to know the truth to be made free? Jesus, by His power, gets rid of the strongman, but by His truth, He breaks down the strongholds in our minds, which results in even greater freedom than removal of unclean spirits.

Anointing drives out demons, the truth breaks down strongholds. We need both. It is not the presence of truth that sets us free, instead, it's the knowledge of truth that brings freedom.

Truth is like soap, it only works once applied. If you have a truck load of soap but, you do not apply it on your skin, it will be useless. Truth in the Bible does not change your life, it is when you intimately know that truth, that by its very nature it starts to bring freedom into your mind.

Truth is more than facts, it is what God says about us. Facts change, truth does not. Truth is eternal. Jesus is the Truth. The more we know Jesus, the more truth we know about ourselves, and the more freedom comes into our mind from strongholds.

This freedom does not come by the touch of Jesus, but by the teaching of Jesus. It is getting God's Word inside of our heart by listening, reading, memorizing, confessing, and obeying it. This will begin to break mental strongholds in our life and give us freedom to move forward with Holy Spirit.

There was one young lady who came to our service and got saved. As I was ministering to her, she mentioned that she had an accident during her pregnancy that caused huge stress, which opened a door to the fear of driving. At that time, she had not driven for four years. It made her life difficult. I prayed for her and cast out the spirit of fear. I felt prompted to ask her to take the Word of God, a verse, 2 Timothy 1:7, and write it down one thousand times. Then after that, get behind the wheel of a car and drive.

The first time I heard of this was from David Cho, who told a lady who was unable to get healed from cancer, to write this promise down one thousand times – "By His stripes we are healed." After she wrote that promise one thousand times, God healed her.

This young lady started to write out this verse daily. The purpose for this was to clear out her mind with the Word of God, from accidents and fears that had come into it.

Our mind is like a ship. Once it gets hit by the icebergs of life, we get holes and the water around us starts to slip inside of us, creating a stronghold. The Titanic did not sink because there was too much water in the ocean, it sunk because the water got inside.

By giving her the assignment of writing down the Scripture, I wanted to get the water of fear out of her soul. She did not even finish writing down the verse one thousand times before she started to drive again and the Lord set her free. Knowing the truth brings freedom.

A God to Pharaoh

Moses was called to deliver Israel from bondage, and God promised His support. When Moses arrived in Egypt and demanded Pharaoh to let God's people go, Pharaoh did not budge. Instead, he made the work of Israel even harder by asking them to produce the same amount of bricks without providing the straw to make them. Pharaoh thought Moses was a joke. Israel thought Moses was crazy, promising their freedom by only making things worse. Moses was upset at God for all of this.

God reassured Moses that everything was going to be okay and went on to say, "See, I have made you as God to Pharaoh, and Aaron your brother shall be your prophet," (Exodus 7:1). Pharaoh did not obey Moses, and Israel did not listen to him either. Moses was disappointed, and God's solution was for Moses to be as God to Pharaoh? Interesting phenomenon. God was showing him something powerful about spiritual warfare. Moses was freed from Egypt, but the slave mentality had to be broken out of him. He no longer could view himself as a slave if he wanted to deliver the other slaves. God wanted him to see himself differently, and God expected him to do that before things changed with Pharaoh and Israel.

God's solution to this situation was not a quick fix, nor did He speed up the process of the exodus. Instead, He revealed the spiritual position of Moses. This required Moses to change how he saw himself in his own eyes. The words, "You are as God to Pharaoh," should not freak you out. Pharaoh saw himself as a god that the Egyptians worshipped, along with other gods. God made it clear to Moses, in the spiritual realm, you are superior and if you want to accomplish the deliverance for Israel, you have to stop begging Pharaoh like a slave. Instead, Moses needed to command him as a boss.

I believe Moses received that revelation, for the evidence was incredible. Pharaoh started to beg Moses to pray that the plagues would stop. He no longer saw Moses as a joke, he was now respected even in the courts of his enemies.

You have to know who you are in Christ if you want to see God's power flow through you. You have the authority of the name of Jesus at your command to execute vengeance on God's enemies, Satan, sin, and sickness. Stop seeing yourself as a slave, otherwise you will live like a slave, even if you have been given freedom from the bondage of sin. This mental shift not only changed Pharaoh's reaction towards Moses, but also facilitated the 10 plagues that were released, which directly attacked the gods of Egypt. The gods of Egypt were shattered.

When the water turned into blood, Hapi, the Egyptian god of the Nile was attacked.

When frogs came out of the Nile River, Heket, the Egyptian goddess of fertility, water, and renewal was attacked.

When lice came from the earth, Geb, the Egyptian god of earth and dust was attacked.

When swarms of flies came, Kherphi, the Egyptian god who had the head of a flea was attacked.

When death of the cattle and livestock occurred, Hathor, the Egyptian goddess who had the head of cow was attacked.

When the ashes turned to boils and sores, Isis, the Egyptian goddess of medicine came crashing down.

When hail rained down in the form of fire, Nut, the Egyptian goddess of the sky was defeated.

When locusts were sent from the sky, Seth, the Egyptian god of storms and disorder was in disarray.

When there were three days of complete darkness, Ra, the sun god, who was the most worshipped god in Egypt other than Pharaoh, gave no light, and was shamed.

When the death of the first born came, Pharaoh was attacked, who was considered the son of Ra, manifested in the flesh, as he was worshipped by Egypt as the greatest Egyptian god of all. An attack came into his own house.[11]

As you can see, Moses had to walk in authority to be victorious over the demonic forces behind these gods. These were not just made up idols that Egypt worshipped. These were demonic entities that could only be defeated by the power of God.

You have to embrace the authority of God if you want to walk in the authority of God. You might not feel it if your life is falling apart right now. Perhaps you have taken a few steps forward and hell is breaking loose. You have to renew your mind to what God says about you and move forward. The Devil has to flee. He has to beg that you leave him alone like he begged Jesus when He came on the earth. Demons do not react to your pain, but only to the authority you walk in.

Jesus stripped away the authority of the forces of darkness, which means they have none, but they will act like they do. You are the policeman and the Devil is a criminal. Criminals run from the police, not the other way around. The Devil has to flee, not you. You have the badge representing the authority of Jesus, and the gun is the power of Holy Spirit. When you know who you are, the forces of darkness will run and you will see God's glory on your life.

Slave, Survivor, or Soldier

Not only did Moses have to adjust his mindset about himself before being used by God to deliver Israel out of Egypt, but Israel had to do the same thing in the wilderness. God wanted to break down the mental strongholds of slavery by taking them through things before they reached the Promised Land.

In Egypt they were slaves, but to possess the Promised Land, they needed to become soldiers. In Egypt, they waited for God to split the sea, but in the Promised Land they walked into the Jordan River and it split. In Egypt, Pharaoh let them go, in the Promised Land they drove out the enemy.

The transition from Egypt to the Promised Land was a mental shift from a slave to a soldier. Most of them did not make it through that transition and died in the wilderness. It was easier for God to get them out of Egypt than to get Egypt out of them. In the same way it was easier for Jesus to expel thousands of demons from a demon possessed person than to break strongholds in the minds of the Pharisees.

God allows the wilderness in our lives to kill the mentality of slavery, poverty, victimization, sickness, and every other mentality that is not in line with God's Word.

In Egypt, we learned how to think like slaves. The wilderness teaches us how to survive, but the Promised Land requires us to think like soldiers. In Egypt, Israel did not have enough. In the wilderness it was just enough, and in the Promised Land there was more than enough. Which mentality do you currently subscribe to? Slave, survivor, or soldier?

A slave mentality is a victim mentality. A survivor mentality is a wilderness mentality. A soldier is a sonship mentality. It is the mentality of the kingdom. The kingdom mentality requires us to work with God, instead of just waiting on God. We do not need to beg for Him to give us what is already ours through Calvary.

The parable of the father and his two sons shows that the older son was waiting for the Father to give him something that was already his. The older son expected the Father to give it to him, just as Israel was expecting that God would do something to the enemies in the Promised Land, as He did to the Egyptians. People with the slave mentality will play the part of the victim and expect God to do everything for them. The older son played the victim role, even though he had all of the inheritance. A mental shift has to take place if we are to see every last stronghold of Egypt destroyed in our lives.

Complete Victory

Joshua, who followed Moses, took the nation of soldiers into the Promised Land. He defeated 31 kings. Half of the book of Joshua is about the defeat of their enemies. The other half is about their dividing the spoils. Anytime you overcome things, a blessing will follow. Some nations were left though, meaning their victory was not complete.

Sometimes, during deliverance, when someone prays for you, you might feel like the victory is not complete. You may receive something from the Lord, especially when someone ministers to you, but you may still feel like it is not complete. Maybe God is trying to give you a jump start and wants you now to fight for the rest of it with Him. The mistake some people make is that they keep seeking another minister, another ministry with deeper anointing, while ignoring their part in fighting and standing on the Word of God. Partial victory was given to them for a reason.

Look at what God said about why some of the enemy stayed, "Now these are the nations which the Lord left, that He might test Israel by them, that is, all who had not known any of the wars in Canaan (this was only so that the generations of the children of Israel might be taught to know war, at least those who had not formerly known it)," (Judges 3:1-2).

God left some enemy kings as a way to see if Israel would still obey God, in spite of their enemies, to help teach them how to fight. I feel like, sometimes, God does not deliver us 100 percent when someone ministers to us, so that there are battles for us to be able to exercise our own spiritual authority for our freedom.

I am reminded of a scene in the movie "The Chronicles of Narnia: The Lion, the Witch, and the Wardrobe," where wolves attacked Peter and Aslan. Aslan did not intervene, but told Peter that it was his turn to learn how to use his sword. Most of us chicken out when things like this happen, and only rely on someone else who is a preacher, or a man of God, to bring about deliverance.

Maybe you've received partial victory. A word of advice, do not sit and wait for more. Go hard after God, press into the kingdom of God, and you will see how that partial victory will turn into complete victory. The best part is that you will become a soldier in the process. This new mindset that you will develop will come in handy for you in your future endeavors with God.

Reign in Life

Like Adam, we were created by God in His image and likeness. We are blessed by God to be fruitful and multiply and are given dominion on the earth (see Genesis 1:28). Dominion over sin and

Satan came as a right for us. It is in our nature to reign, just as it is in its nature for a bird to fly and for a fish to swim. We were not created for deliverance, we were created for dominion. Deliverance came as result of failing to exercise our dominion. God wanted man to be like Him. God rules the heavens and He gave dominion over earth to man (see Psalm 115:16). God did not give man ownership of the earth, only dominion (see Psalm 24:1). This was expressed when God let Adam name the animals, since naming something meant claiming it.

God gave us dominion over the earth. He entrusted us to rule over our enemy. Paradise on earth is not the absence of the Devil, but dominion over him. In order to have dominion, we need to have an enemy. Adam failed to kill the snake, instead, he listened to it. When Adam committed sin, God did not take over the earth, Satan did. Through sin, Adam transferred his dominion to the Devil, that is why the Devil could offer the world to Jesus during temptation (see Matthew 4:9). God never gave the world to the Devil. The world was given to men to rule, but through sin, that rulership was transferred over to the Devil. Even Jesus confirmed this by calling Satan "the ruler of this world," (see John 12:31).

The mess on earth is a direct result of man's mismanagement, or lack of dominion, over the forces of darkness and sin. Jesus came to take that authority from the Devil and give it back to us (see Luke 10:19). You would think God saw how we blew it the first time, and would not trust us again with dominion. God has more faith in us than we do in Him. He trusts us to expand His Kingdom, cast out the kingdom of darkness, and trample upon the old dragon.

Deliverance is not the goal of God, instead it is the means to get us back into our rightful place of authority, which is dominion. "For if by the one man's offense death reigned through the one, much more those who receive abundance of grace and of the gift of righteousness will reign in life through the One, Jesus Christ,"

(Romans 5:17). God's grace and gift of righteousness is to help us reign in life, not just get free from sin and the Devil. Your ability to reign and rule is proportional to your revelation of the gift of Jesus' righteousness and abundance of His grace.

Satan rules over us because of our sin, but we can rule over him, because of righteousness and grace. Do not settle for deliverance from sin. Go to God's original intent for you which is dominion and to reign in life. Grace is not given to us to make us merely survive, but to thrive.

Prayer

"Lord Jesus, I thank You for giving me the gift of righteousness and abundance of grace, so that I will not just survive, but thrive in my life. I accept Your truth in me, to walk in victory and dominion. I renew my mind in accordance with Your truth about who I am in the spiritual world. I invite Your truth to change my mindset from lack to abundance, from mess to miracles, and from fear to faith."

CHAPTER 10

RENEWING OF THE MIND

During my birth, my mother had a difficult time. I was told that a part of my optical nerve was damaged in the process of birth, and I had to spend quite some time in the hospital during my infancy. However, by God's mercy and grace, I came out as a healthy child. Years later, they started to notice that one eye lid was weaker than the other, and that one of my eyes would not look up when the other one would. As a child, I do not remember that being a problem. I saw perfectly and had no pain in my eyes.

Before coming to the United States when I was about 10 years of age, a doctor in Ukraine performed my first eye surgery. It was supposed to help my weak eye to be able look up when the other eye would look up. The surgery did not do much, and the problem still remained. At school, when I was still in the Ukraine, I was given a nickname which referred to my eyes. I started to feel like a deformed child.

These feelings became strongest when our family moved to the USA. I was 13-years-old. I became more closed in and embarrassed to be around people. I had great difficulty socializing, and I avoided birthday parties at all cost. I even skipped classes out of shame, because I didn't want to stand in front of people for presentations. I felt as if God had made a mistake when He made me. I thought the world would have been a better place without me in it. Because I grew up in a godly family with strong parents, I would never contemplate taking my own life, but I did wish for God to create an accident that would kill me, just to relieve myself of the pain.

I used to meet people who asked me this question, "What happened to your eyes?" It made me feel so terrible. I felt like that was the only thing they could see about me. When I was around others, I could sense that they were not very comfortable around me. I believed it was people's fault for rejecting me and God's fault for making me like that.

So, I prayed for healing for my eyes, thinking if my physical body changed, my mental feelings would change as well. I had one more surgery in the USA, hoping that it would change my appearance. Unfortunately, it did not do anything. However, I am going to share with you what did change.

My mind changed. Being a teenager, I channeled these hurts and inner pains by going to prayer. I would spend 30-45 minutes every week day after school in my room praying and worshipping, and then I would read the Word of God. I would read Christian books and listen to sermons on cassettes (there were no podcasts or YouTube at that time). I would take every Wednesday to fast and feed on the Bible, at times reading up to 50 chapters a day.

Slowly, but surely, the words of God, along with the help of the Spirit of God, were becoming alive in me. Layer by layer, the lies were being removed and replaced with the truth. My grades improved in school, I was no longer embarrassed by people or afraid of public speaking. People's reaction towards me also changed. Today, when I speak or meet people, they do not ask me about my eyes, and most people do not care. The reason they are not bothered is because it does not bother me. I learned that the renewing of the mind transforms your life.

Come Out Head First

The Apostle Paul said in Romans 12:2 that we are transformed by the renewing of the mind. Many of us think that once our life is transformed, then our mind will be renewed. It is actually the other way around. When we were born, most of us came out of the womb, and into this world, head first. If you want to come out of unpleasant circumstances, limitation in career, stagnation in your ministry, your head has to come out first.

When your mind is changed, your life will be transformed. Remember, where your mind goes, your life follows. When you experience deliverance, your mind has to switch from a slave to a son, from a slave to a soldier. Even if you get the same attacks as before, you get to see them from a different position. I like to tell our church, "You are not a sick person trying to get healed, you are healthy person fighting sickness." "You are not a bound person trying to get free, you are a free person fighting bondage." "You are not a sinner trying to get holy, you are a saint fighting sin."

Sickness, sin, and bondage are not my identity. I am in Christ now — that is my new identity — and whatever I am facing, I will overcome because of my position in Him.

First the Light and Then the Sun

God moves by faith and faith involves the way we think. Holy Spirit moves in our life through a renewed mind. God set that as the pattern in the beginning when creating the earth. "The earth was without form, and void; and darkness was on the face of the deep. And the Spirit of God was hovering over the face of the waters," (Genesis 1:2). The state of the earth was void and dark, without form. Maybe that is the state of your life right now – empty, dark, and without form. As it was with the Earth, so it is with you as a Christian. Even though Holy Spirit was present, nothing was changing, there was still no form, it was just void and dark. Holy Spirit did not do the miracle of creation until God sent a word.

As I mentioned before, the renewing of the mind does not happen outside of truth. Holy Spirit uses the truth as a means by which He brings change in our minds, and the result is a transformation in our lives. "Then God said, 'Let there be light'; and there was light. And God saw the light, that it was good; and God divided the light from the darkness. God called the light Day, and the darkness He called Night. So the evening and the morning were the first day," (Genesis 1:3).

On the first day, God first created light. When I was younger and did not read the Bible carefully, I was under the impression that God created the sun, the moon, and the stars on the first day, since He created light. As I grew in age and faith, and read the Bible more carefully, I realized that the sun, moon and stars were created on day four (see Genesis 1:14-19). The question arises, where did the light come from on day one if the sun, moon and stars came on day four?

In the natural world, you cannot have light without the sun. God demonstrated something from the first few verses of the Bible that is contrary to our natural way of seeing things. In our world we cannot have light without the sun. In God's world, you cannot have the sun without the light. In our world, you cannot be a father until you have children. In God's world, you become a father and then you get children. (For example, Abraham receiving a name as a father before having children.) In our world, we fight to get victory. In God's world, we receive victory, therefore we fight. In our world, we become righteous after we have done right things. In God's world, we become righteous first, so that we can do right deeds. Often, when our lives change, then our mood and thinking changes, but in God's world, first our minds have to change and then our lives change.

As you see God thinks differently than us. If we want to work with God, we must think more like Him. If the light did not come from the sun, then where did it come from? The answer is simple, "Then God said," (Genesis 1:3). God's word created the light before the sun. God's word created something that should not be there without the sun, moon or stars. Most of us are praying for God to give us the sun. Our sun may come in the form of healing, breakthrough, or salvation a loved one. Sometimes, we are defeated on the inside, full of negativity, doubt, and fear. We are convinced that if God would only bring a miracle in our lives, then our emotional and mental state would change right away.

Have you ever thought that maybe God is trying to bring the miracle in your mind, first, by the power of His Word and Spirit? The story about the creation of the world teaches us that before there can be sun in our lives, there has to be light in our minds. Your mind must be already filled with the reality of the miracle, even though it is not in your circumstances yet. God's word has to become so real in your spirit that it changes your inner world, as though you have already received the desired outcome in your life. The Word of God is not given to you to fill your mind with information, instead, it is given to you so that Holy Spirit can use it to bring revelation. Simply put, the Word of God becomes so real that it changes how you think and what you feel.

Faith is not Hoping, it is Having

Your whole world changes if you let God's Word change your mind and soul. People suffer in their circumstances as a result of wrong thinking. Many pray more, but in reality, freedom from mental strongholds is achieved through the truth of God's Word, not just praying more for deliverance.

My wife and I have a goal to give a car away once a year. We started this four years ago, and as of 2018, we have given away six cars. It is not because we are rich, but because we believe that God wants us to be more known for our generosity than our wealth. The

123

second car we gave away was a nice Toyota Camry. We decided to bless a couple in our church who were about to have their first child, and they had just gone through an accident, losing their vehicle. We knew that they were looking for a car, so without delaying we quickly gave them the car. We made that decision on Saturday. The following day, Sunday, we invited them to lunch and announced that we wanted to bless them with our vehicle. They broke down, it was unreal for them. At that time this car was worth about $10,000. It was a pretty great gift. We told them that we would give them the keys to the car a little later since I wanted to change the bumper, change the oil, and fix a few things to make it the best gift possible.

After they heard this news, they left our home as owners of the car, even though they did not get to drive the car home. They did not get the car or the keys, just a promise, and this promise made them sure that the car was theirs. They stopped shopping or worrying about a vehicle. They knew they had a nice car and it was coming. What made them possess the car on the inside? My promise, my word.

That is how God wants us to take Him at His promise. He wants to create a new reality inside of you based on what He says. Later on, He will bring that reality on the outside of your life.

A month later, during Friday night prayer, I handed them the paperwork and the keys. They finally drove the car that day, but they actually got the car when I gave them that promise. Faith is not hoping for something to happen, it is having it inside of you before it manifests on the outside. That is the power of a renewed mind.

Faith is the Title Deed

"Now faith is the substance of things hoped for, the evidence of things not seen," (Hebrews 11:1). The word substance is from the Greek word "hypostatis" which simply means 'title deed'. When you get the title deed for property or a car, you become the owner of it, even if you physically do not have it yet. By the power of God's Word, the Holy Spirit makes the promise real within you and you become the owner of the things promised.

Doubt sees what you have and nothing else. Hope sees what is possible based on the general Word of God. Faith is the personal reality of this promise, made real through hearing it in our heart, from God. A renewed mind and faith go together to break the mental barriers in our lives that hold us back from our full freedom in God.

When God starts to work inside of you, this will produce new thoughts, feelings, and attitudes. Even if your life is not changing, do not stop believing and holding onto God's truth. His truth is so much more powerful than facts. Facts will change, truth remains eternal. If God has brought Day One into your life by bringing about light into your mind, rest assured, there will be a Day Four where you will see the miracle of the sun, moon and stars. Remember, you can only be in health and prosper as your soul prospers (see 3 John 1:2). God wants real change and breakthrough to begin from the inside and to overflow into your health, finances, and relationships.

First Step for Renewing Your Mind

Stop waiting for an outside miracle to change your mind. Most of those miracles will never come until you get rid of the chaos in your mind by filling it with God's Word. Renewing of the mind will never work if someone believes this excuse, "The reason why my mind is so negative is because my life is so hard." Have you ever thought that maybe the reason your life is so hard is because your mind is so negative? You cannot have miracles in your life regularly if your mind is a mess.

Stop making your mind a sidewalk for the Devil to trample on, make it a disciple to the Word of God. The type of ground where the birds stole the seed was along the path (see Matthew 13:4). Do not let the Devil walk on your mind as a sidewalk, otherwise the Word of God has no chance to bring change. The birds will steal it from your heart.

Israel thought that more miracles will change their minds, but most of them died as victims in the wilderness, even though they witnessed more miracles than any other generation will have a chance to see. The Pharisees believed this same lie, that if Jesus would do a few more miracles, then they would believe He was the Son of God. In spite of all the supernatural things Jesus did, including the resurrection of the dead, they still remained unconvinced.

Do not get me wrong, we need miracles, but they alone do not change our minds without our humility and willingness to make God's Word the standard for our lives. Remember, the same sun that melts the ice also hardens the clay. Miracles are like that—for those who are hungry for God's Word, miracles help our faith, but for those who are refusing God's Word to have dominion over their lives, miracles are never enough. If you stop blaming your circumstances for your negative thinking, God will start working on you in a powerful way.

Second Step for Renewing Your Mind

Stop believing that you can't control your thoughts. The second lie that must be repented of is, I cannot control my thoughts, they control me. It is a weak excuse, and this excuse is not Scriptural. The Bible commands us to "Think about these things," (Philippians 4:8), "You shall meditate on it day and night," (Joshua 1:8), "On His law he meditates day and night," (Psalm 1:2).

It is pretty clear that you are expected by God to choose your thoughts, not let your thoughts always be chosen by something else. How do we do this practically? It is true that we get attacked in our minds, because our minds are a battlefield, not a playground. As a Christian begins to connect his spirit with Holy Spirit, his spirit begins to get stronger.

The mind is a servant, either to your spirit or to your flesh. When the spirit is weak, the mind runs errands for the flesh by thinking negative thoughts. But when we constantly build our spirit by communion with Holy Spirit, our mind comes under the influence of the Word of God and Holy Spirit who lives in us. We are left with the choice to think on God's things or let the mind go with the flow of life.

Every country has border patrol to stop people from entering who are not supposed to enter. It is for the protection and safety of the country. You have to set up a border control in your mind to stop all terrorist thoughts of doubt, fear, and negativity from entering and living in your mind. They only bring harm to your life.

Third Step for Renewing Your Mind

What you feed your mind with becomes a mindset. A mindset is impossible to change without changing what your mind is filled with. Typically, when we hear the truth about breaking strongholds or renewing of the mind, we get busy trying to change our mindsets. We quickly learn that it is not an easy task.

A mindset is what controls you. The mind is what you control. The only way to change your default and automatic thinking is by filling your conscious mind with new information of God's truth. Once the conscious mind is filled to the overflow, it slips into the subconscious mind.

Ninety-five percent of our behaviors are automatic, that is why we set goals, but do not reach them. Setting goals is the function of the conscious mind, but reaching them is the task of the subconscious mind. The subconscious mind occupies most of your brain. It does not work by logic, therefore, it believes anything that it is told repeatedly by the conscious mind.

It is important that we feed our minds with information from the Word of God. Holy Spirit turns that information, which we fed our mind with, into revelation, and this soon becomes our new mindset. Every time you give an opportunity for Holy Spirit to bring revelation out of the information of God's Word, you can be sure that He will turn the revelation of that Word into manifestation of that Word. And then His Word will produce visible results in your life.

Before there can be manifestation in your circumstances, you must allow the Spirit of God to bring revelation into your spirit.

Lastly, before there can be revelation by the Spirit, you must fill your mind with information from God's Word as much as possible. Read, memorize, and meditate on the Bible, listen to podcasts, and read Christian books. Fill your mind with the truth, and Holy Spirit will make it come alive which will change your mindset and transform your life.

Fourth Step for Renewing Your Mind

Confess what you believe, not what you feel. We possess what we confess. We possess salvation by confessing Jesus as Lord of our lives. We possess God's promises by confessing them with our mouths. When you regularly confess only what you feel and see, you are hurting your faith and not helping negative thoughts to leave.

When God saw the world in darkness, void, and without form – He did not use His words to describe the situation. Instead He used the power of His word to change the situation. Don't use your mouth as a thermometer, which only reads the temperature of your current condition, allow God's word to turn your mouth into a thermostat, which changes the temperature of your life by confessing what God says.

The Lord instructed Joshua, "This book of the law shall not depart from your mouth," (Joshua 1:8). Joshua had to not only read the book, or study it, but also speak it. Jesus did that in the wilderness in His temptation with the Devil. Most likely the Devil tempted Jesus as he usually tempts us, with thoughts. Jesus did not think the Scripture to combat the Devil's arrows, He spoke the Scripture.

It's so powerful when evil thoughts attack your mind to open your mouth and speak in line with God's Word, not your feelings or current circumstances. As it says in Joel 3:10, "Let the weak say, 'I am strong.'" Don't speak what you feel all the time, otherwise your mind can't change. Learn to speak God's word instead.

Fifth Step for Renewing Your Mind

Resist negative thoughts, assist positive thoughts. Positive thoughts are not going to stay, they need to be assisted. Negative thoughts are not going to leave, they need to be resisted.

The first parable of Jesus about the seed, soil, and the sower in Matthew 13 shows that bad things like weeds need to be pulled out and good seeds need to be planted. All good seeds need nurturing for them to sprout. For the bad seed to grow, you need to do nothing. It grows on its own. Good seeds, unfortunately, do not grow like that. The same goes with thoughts. Bad ones will not leave; good ones will not stay.

We must assist the Word of God by making room for it in our hearts, and resist the evil thoughts of the enemy by taking them captive and bringing them into submission to Christ (see 2 Corinthians 10:5).

The Bible describes the mind as a ship looking for harbor. You cannot keep bad ships from sailing back and forth on the ocean, but you can refuse them from docking privileges in the harbor of your mind (see Jeremiah 4:14; Deuteronomy 15:9).

You cannot stop birds from flying over your head, but you can stop them from building a nest in your hair. Bad thoughts come, but do not have to stay if we speak against them with the truth of God's Word.

Sixth Step for Renewing Your Mind

Celebrate the process. It is going to take time to see change in your mind. I think there is a reason why God took six days to create the world instead of one day. He wanted to show us how to go through the process of change.

Each day something great was done and God would end the day by celebrating what was done, instead of complaining about what was still not done. On the third day, when there was still so much work to be done, God saw that it was good. God did not look at what still was unfinished. Much was yet to be done but He celebrated what was complete.

Renewing of the mind happens when we celebrate small victories and focus on what God is doing, instead of what He is not doing. Also, it is worthy to note that God never compared the messy process of creation to the beautiful heaven where He resides.

The Devil will try to mess up the process of your mind renewal by making you compare your progress with someone else.

We are all on different days of creation. We must fix our eyes on the Creator and not compare ourselves with others. Comparing kills contentment. We are encouraged to run the race looking to Jesus, not to another runner to see how we compare with another's journey. The greatest joy in life is to know who you are and who you are not, to be comfortable in your own skin and happy with the path that God has you on, even if it looks like you are way behind everyone else.

You are complete in God. You do not need to compare yourself to others. Comparing leads to complaining. Complaining can lead to breaking the 10th commandment of coveting. Coveting kills the creative process of God in renewing your mind.

If your neighbor's lawn looks greener than yours, start watering your own lawn. Be the best version of you the world has ever seen. Remember, what God started, He is faithful to finish (see Philippians 1:6). He is not done with you yet.

Seventh Step for Renewing Your Mind

Expect miracles. Expecting something good to happen is a choice. It is an act of our faith. A person with a renewed mind has positive expectations in the forefront of their mind. Do not let your imagination create an image in which things will go bad for you, such as sickness worsening, relationships breaking, business failing, etc. Replace those negative imaginations with promises from God's Word.

There is a funny story of a young couple who got married and the wife kept getting this feeling that someone was in the house trying to rob them. She would ask her husband to go and check on the house. He would check the house and find no one there. This continued week after week for a long time, until he got tired of getting up and checking on the house, only to find it safe and secure. But out of respect for his wife, he would still go and check on the house. One time during a nightly routine check at the request of his wife, he was surprised to see a thief in the house. The robber told him not to make any noise and to give him all the valuables. After the husband gave him what he demanded, before the thief would leave, he asked the robber not to leave so soon, but to meet his wife, since she had been expecting him for all those years.

Expectations are a breeding place for miracles. Some people wake up in the morning with a feeling that something bad is going to happen to them that day. If that happens to you, it is from the Devil. Go back to bed and wake up again until you have a positive feeling that God is good and He plans good things.

If you keep getting bad thoughts that something will happen and they do, you are releasing your faith for your own trouble. I choose to trust in God and expect His grace and mercy, not accidents, tickets, or all hell breaking loose.

Does that mean we will never have bad days? No! But we will not live expecting them.

Prayer

"Precious Holy Spirit, You are hovering over my life right now. All I can see is darkness, all I can feel is void in my life. I accept Your word as the final authority in my life. I ask that You will take the information from the Bible and make it a revelation in my heart. Oh, Holy Spirit, bring the manifestation of God's Word into my life. Let my reality rise to the level of Your truth."

CHAPTER 11

STAY ON FIRE

There was a rich man who was looking for a driver for his family. This happened back in the day when drivers drove horse-drawn carriages. This wealthy man decided to let three candidates show their skills for the job. He brought them to a steep cliff and had them drive the empty carriage by the cliff.

The first driver drove the horse-drawn carriage as close to the cliff as he possibly could. Everyone was impressed.

The second driver went even closer to the cliff to the point that one wheel was hanging over the cliff as he drove the carriage. Certainly, no one could beat that, his family thought.

The third driver drove as far as possible from the cliff. He explained that when he would drive the family of the rich man, it would be best to keep them as far from danger as possible. He got the job.

In our walk with Christ, there are two types of people. One comes as close to the line of the cliff as possible and the other tries to go as far as possible from the cliff of sin and stay closer to Jesus. Questions that youth ask these days when it comes to sexual sin is, "How far is too far?" or, "Where is the line?" These questions reveal that our generation is not interested in staying closer to God, but it wants to see how close to hell it can get without going there!

I always tell young people that they are asking the wrong question. Let's imagine that I know God's Word says that adultery is wrong. That is the cliff I want to avoid in my marriage. I come to my wife and ask, is it okay for me to hang out with another woman?

Text another woman all the time? Maybe hold hands in public? Kiss her good night? Maybe sleep with her without having sex? What do you think my wife would say? Would her reaction be – yes, you can do all of that as long as you do not cross the line of adultery?

It would be the opposite – my wife would be furious that I asked these questions. Instead, my goal and questions should focus on how close I can get to her, not how close can I get to the cliff of adultery without falling into divorce. God wants us to prioritize pursuing Him more than avoiding the cliff of compromise.

Avoiding the Ditch

Nobody commits completely wrong choices without making unwise decisions along the way. The reason we excuse unwise actions is because they are usually not wrong. If you want to avoid ending up in the ditch of sin, you must avoid getting on the white line of unwise decisions.

Remember, most unwise decisions are not always sinful, therefore, we give ourselves an excuse to come as close to sin as we possibly can but soon it becomes too late.

When David committed adultery, it was wrong, and led to the sin of murder. Adultery did not just happen. It was a result of multiple unwise decisions. David crossed the line, and the rumble strip, before he plunged into adultery.

When it was time for kings to go to war, David was anointed to lead Israel into war, but he decided to stay home. Was it wrong for David not to go to war? I do not think so! But it was unwise for him to stay home when his army was on the battle field. Unwise decisions lead to more unwise decisions. David stayed home and, "Then it happened one evening that David arose from his bed and walked on the roof of the king's house," (2 Samuel 11:2). Understand this, David stayed home, slept all day, and got out of bed in the evening. I know he was in a position of a king, but sleeping all day is not wise. It is not wrong, but it is also not wise for a king.

One unwise decision led to another and then he saw a woman bathing. It was a natural thing for a person to do during that time. There was nothing specifically wrong with him seeing that. Where he went wrong was beholding her and then inviting her to his house. David got stuck in the ditch of more lies, deceit, and destruction that cost him dearly. If you want to avoid falling into your past sins again, avoid doing things that are not wise.

Foolish Virgins

Remember the story about the ten virgins? Half of them were wise and the other half were foolish (see Matthew 25). The five foolish virgins did not lose their virginity. They did not do anything wrong, but they did what was unwise. Doing that led them to the huge disappointment of missing an appointment toward their destiny. Not losing your "virginity" is not a guarantee you will reach your fullest potential.

God wants us to live wisely by staying away from things that lead to sin. The best way to stay far from sin is by keeping a great distance from things that are, in and of themselves, not considered to be sinful, but which when participated in, will lead us to sin.

The man who built his house on the sand was not wrong, but he was called unwise. When your moral compass is built on trying to only avoid doing what is wrong, you might fall apart sooner or later. The wise man built his house on the rock. If you want your integrity and freedom to outdo storms and temptations, build your convictions around avoiding unwise decisions, not just wrong choices.

Flirting Leads to Falling

Joseph was tempted in the house of Potiphar day after day. We do not see him flirting with the wife of that man or spending time with her. He was a single man who had rough years in his youth. His family already had a death certificate for him, for them he did not exist. He was a slave, and his dreams were on pause. This was a great excuse to flirt with sin. Joseph did not have a pastor, church, or the Bible to steer him in the right path. Yet, he did better with fighting sin than most of us, today. His principle was simple, if you want to avoid falling into sin, you cannot flirt with it.

Do not flirt, flee! Everyone who falls into sin, first flirts with it. The excuse we use for flirting is that it is not actually committing the sin. Well, you do not fall until you flirt. Some use God's grace as an excuse to flirt with sin. Grace was given to us to give us power to run from sin, not play with it.

"For the grace of God that brings salvation has appeared to all men, teaching us that, denying ungodliness and worldly lusts, we should live soberly, righteously, and godly in the present age," (Titus 2:11-12). Grace is more than a giver of salvation. It is a teacher that teaches us how to deny ungodliness and worldly lusts, and live differently in this world.

"For you, brethren, have been called to liberty; only do not use liberty as an opportunity for the flesh, but through love serve one another," (Galatians 5:13). Let's not use our freedom as an excuse to flirt with those things which could lead us back into bondage faster than we can imagine.

Loins Girded and Lamps Burning

The reason why we need to stay away from unwise things, or from the edge, is not only limited to our avoiding falling into sin. It also gives us a passion for the pursuit of God.

"Let your waist be girded and your lamps burning," (Luke 12:35). This is the challenge of Jesus for the people in the last days. Put a belt on your waist, which means tighten your convictions. If you do things that lead to sin, yet you are trying to avoid falling into sin – your convictions are loosed and very soon your pants will fall off, meaning your freedom will be lost again. Strong convictions hold your freedom. When convictions are loosed, we compromise which leads us to losing what we received from the Lord.

Girded loins and strong convictions hold our robes together, but also this is what gives us a chance for our lamps to be burning. When you stop running from sin, it comes with a price—you will stop running after God. Both elements are connected, loins and lamps are intertwined. Purity and passion are associated. Each needs the other. Convictions hold our freedom; our freedom allows us to run after God undistracted.

Throw the Snake into Your Fire

When walking in wisdom, convictions protect us from falling into sin, but it does not protect us from being tempted or from being attacked.

"But when Paul had gathered a bundle of sticks and laid them on the fire, a viper came out because of the heat, and fastened on his hand...But he shook off the creature into the fire and suffered no harm" (Acts 28:3, 5). Paul was on the path of righteousness, following God and staying close to Holy Spirit, not flirting with sin. Yet, he experienced a storm, a shipwreck, and then he was faced with a snake. God gave him grace to survive the storm and the shipwreck, but when it came to the snake, something else happened.

While it was raining, Paul gathered sticks to build a fire. An interesting lesson was learned here – don't let your storm and your shipwreck make you passive, or stop you from kindling fire within your soul for the Lord. Do not let past drama and trauma make you cold towards God and retreat into living on the memories of the good old days. God wants you to burn today, for He is the Great I Am, not the Great I Was. If you remember a time when you loved Jesus more than today, you have backslidden. It is time to build that fire again in your life. Do not use what people did and what you have been through as an excuse to freeze in the cold. Your enemies might have taken your past, but it is with your permission that they kill your passion in the present.

Truly, it is not easy to start a fire in the rain. Keeping passion alive is not simple after going through different life scenarios. Putting a bundle of sticks together takes some effort. Start disciplining yourself by daily reading the Word, praying, fasting regularly, listening to podcasts and/or messages on YouTube. Spend less time watching television and more time watching testimonies; less time on social media, but more time attending your small group; less time arguing and more time witnessing about your faith. When you do this, you will be amazed how these small sticks bundled together produce fire. It might be a small fire, but it is yours and it is real.

When fire is burning in your life, everything is amazing, even if it comes after a storm and a shipwreck. But wait, this fire in Paul's life exposed a snake. That snake came out and did not just attack Paul, but fastened onto his hand with the intent to stay there and kill him. It's crazy how often this happens when you start living out your Christian faith, walking in freedom, and burning for the Lord. Boom! Out of nowhere, you fall or something hits you – and the snake bites you hard, not letting go.

The snake comes with voices. When the snake bit Paul, people started to talk. "He must be a murderer," someone said. "God is punishing him," another said. "He escaped the storm and the shipwreck, but now fate has gotten him," someone else thought.

When you get attacked like that, and even if you fall into the same sin as you were delivered from, don't listen to the lies of the Devil. His lies are more dangerous than the sin that you fell into again.

Instead of debating with people, Paul shook off the snake into the fire he helped build. The snake died and people started saying he was a god. Opinions of people change so quickly. One moment they said he was a murderer and, in another moment, they said he was a god. Both statements were wrong. We must trust the Word of God more than the opinion of people. On the same note, we must take in the Word of God more than any voices in our head.

Learn to shake off the guilt, shame, and lies when you are attacked. The Devil wants to kill your fire. What you ought to do instead is throw those temptations and trials into the fire, and they will die. Do not stop burning and doing what you were doing before the attack. That is what the Devil wants.

One of the reasons why people die from spiritual snake bites is because they do not have enough of a fire in their life to throw that viper into. You cannot throw your issues into my firepit, you need to build your own. You cannot throw your viper into your pastor's fire, you have to have your own. Turn your heart into a fireplace, stop making it a trashcan where anything and everything goes. You are a temple of Holy Spirit, not a tomb for a dead man's bones. You are called to be a voice, not an echo to your generation.

Revival broke out on the island after the snake died. The Devil wanted to kill Paul so that he could prevent revival, but Paul killed the snake and revival broke out. Every Devil you beat will open up a new level in your personal life. What the Devil means for evil, God will turn around and use it for your good.

Prayer

"Lord Jesus, I want to want You more. I understand that my desire for following You is weak. Holy Spirit, produce within me a desire to follow Jesus. Surround me, Lord, with people who will help me to run this race. Father God, give me Your grace to turn my back on sin and anything leading to sin."

CHAPTER 12

AS YOU GROW

When I was a small boy in Ukraine, my family had a cow, pigs, chickens, and a little garden where we grew most of our food. I grew up knowing how to milk a cow, work in the fields, and take care of our animals.

I was very observant as a young boy to how nature and the animal kingdom works. I especially paid close attention to the hatching of chicks. The mother hen would produce eggs and place them in a safe, comfortable environment. She would sit on those eggs for some time. Later, I learned it was around 21 days. As she would sit and incubate those eggs, on the inside of each egg little chickens were being developed.

Right before the chicks would come out, I could already see darker parts on the shell, indicating something was about to hatch out from the shell. I was surprised to see that the mother hen would not break the shell for her chicks to come out into the new world. She just kept incubating them, keeping them warm. As they kept growing inside, they would outgrow the shell and hatch out of it.

Jesus referred to Himself as a mother hen when talking to Jerusalem. "How often I wanted to gather your children together, as a hen gathers her chicks under her wings, but you were not willing!" (Matthew 23:37). Sometimes, Jesus brings about freedom and change in our lives by the process of our growth in Him. He wants to incubate us, surrounding us with His love, so we can hatch. Not all freedom comes by one prayer, some comes by growing in God. I like to tell our church all the time – some people get delivered at the prayer line, and many will get freed in their prayer life. There are things that only come by growth.

Freedom by Growth

"There is no fear in love; but perfect love casts out fear…" (1 John 4:18). The word "perfect" can be translated as grown up or mature love. There are some things that can be cast out by our maturity in God's love. Fear and love co-exist if love is not mature in you. Once you grow in the Lord, certain things get cast out by your growth. Just as a chicken in the shell keeps growing, it then outgrows the shell and breaks it. Whatever shell of fear you have around you, it will be broken, if you grow in God's love and His Word.

At times we want God to break the shell of our limitations, but despite the afflictions, He desires that we continue to mature in Him. As we grow, our chains begin to break. We outgrow them. So many people give up too soon. They come to the prayer line or counseling for deliverance, nothing happens and they give up on God. Be like the little chicken – stay under the warmth of the hen, do not roll out of the nest, you will see how that which holds you today, shortly will crack and break.

"I will not drive them out from before you in one year, lest the land become desolate and the beasts of the field become too numerous for you. Little by little I will drive them out from before you, until you have increased, and you inherit the land," (Exodus 23:29). Israel did not occupy the Promised Land all at once. Little by little, God would drive their enemies out, until Israel increased to inherit it. God wants you to increase and grow in Him, since your fullest potential and freedom depends on it.

Break the Bands

Scripture compares a righteous man to a palm tree (see Psalm 92:12-15). Palms are a symbol of beauty, which are always green and do not burn in the fire. Like a righteous man, we will not burn in the lake of fire, we will remain always joyful in the Lord, because our roots are planted deep in God.

Palm trees are usually planted in tropical areas. They are not afraid of drought because their roots are very deep. You and I are like that – our surroundings do not determine if we flourish or not, our relationship with God does.

A palm tree withstands abuse, because its strength is in its core, not in its bark. Believers reflect this by living their life from the inside out, instead of outside in. Our strength lies in the Lord, not in how people treat us or how we feel.

A palm tree bends during a storm therefore it does not break. Storms are unavoidable. They come to the wise and foolish. We must not fear storms, if we know how to bend our knees in humility, depending on God. When you bend during a storm like a palm tree, you will not break. Storms will pass and you will rise up again.

There are many comparisons between a palm tree and a righteous person. One thing to highlight is that a palm tree has bands around it, which do not let it grow within. When a palm tree is young, ropes are put around it to help it grow straight. Most trees have ropes that grow into the trees, as the tree is growing. A palm tree is different. Once it grows, the chain that is put on it when it is young, will not let it grow into the tree, instead the chain will break. Imagine the power of the growth of a palm tree.

You are like a palm tree. Maybe the Devil put chains around you when you were weak. Maybe you tried to pray, fast, and do everything to break it, and keep finding yourself stuck in the bands.

The enemy will try his best to convince you that this is how you will be and the issue is your identity—if you cannot beat it, then accept it.

I remember the first case of homosexuality I dealt with as a youth pastor. One young man openly practiced homosexuality and had a boyfriend at that time. He came to our youth gathering. I preached about the woman with the issue of blood and how Jesus called her. My whole point of the message was your issue is not your identity and you cannot be free from it until you stop believing this is who you are.

He approached me after service, asking to meet up and talk. As we sat to talk, he confessed that he had accepted homosexuality as his identity for a long time. I asked him why? Since he grew up in church, he knew from the Bible that God did not make him like that. His response was, "I tried to be free for so long, I prayed, I fasted, I confessed and the same sex attraction was not removed, so I gave up." That night he realized that he had believed a lie. Because he was tired and worn out from the fighting, it was easy to believe the lie.

Remember, you cannot break a band around your life if you let it grow into you and define who you are. Your current issue is not your identity. You are in Christ—that is your identity, who you identify with now. Your identity is in Christ, not in the crisis. Get your head out of the Devil's lie. It is his last attempt to let the chain grow into you, so that you stay like that. Do not believe his lies. You are like a palm tree. During the period of growth, do not let ropes grow into you, they will break slowly, but surely. It may be a process, but you will become stronger as a result. The new strength God will develop in you will be handy for your future victories. Your current battle with the lion and bear will put you in position for great victory against your Goliath.

Anointing will break the yoke. Chains should not become part of who you are. They will be broken if you refuse to let them be grafted into your identity. There is freedom that comes by growing. As you get stronger, things will break! Freedom from fear and other issues are not the only things that come during the process. Anxiety can get broken in the process as well.

Find Rest by Learning

"Come to Me, all you who labor and are heavy laden, and I will give you rest. Take My yoke upon you and learn from Me, for I am gentle and lowly in heart, and you will find rest for your souls," (Matthew 11:28-29). Jesus offers rest for those who come to Him. Rest from the yoke of trying to earn salvation. This is an incredible blessing. Rest is given. We are then commanded to take His yoke and start learning from Him and we will find rest for our souls. There is rest that comes when you come to Jesus, but there is also a rest that comes after you grow in Jesus.

If you did not get complete freedom from depression, anxiety, and heaviness by coming to prayer, the Lord wants you to grow in Him. This growth will result in you finding the rest you need. Not everything comes to us at once. We do not receive all God has for us when we get saved or prayed over for deliverance. Please do not get me wrong – all this is available in Christ to us when we get saved, but some things only come with growing in Christ. There is freedom that Jesus gives and there is freedom that you find.

For example, if your parents bought you a car when you were 10 years of age, you would not be able to drive it legally until you are at least 16 years of age. Growth is necessary to receive what is yours. I believe God spreads out our blessings so that we grow in Him, not just come, get what we need, and leave.

To grow in Jesus, He says, "take My yoke," – this speaks of a covenant with Him. You are equally yoked with Jesus, the King. You are in relationship with Him. This relationship is a covenant – like a marriage. When I got married to my wife, she took on my last name. All that I had became hers and all that she had also became mine. This is like our relationship with Jesus. When we get saved, we get yoked in a covenant with Him. Our battle becomes His and His peace becomes ours. He takes what is ours and gives us what is His.

To grow in Jesus, He says to learn from Him. Jesus teaches us the power of learning. To grow is to learn, to learn is to grow. We can all learn from books, schools, teachers, pastors, but here Jesus says to study Him. Learn who He is – this brings freedom. It goes in line with John 8:32, "And you shall know the truth, and the truth shall make you free."

Later on, Jesus reveals that He is the truth (see John 14:6). As we know Him, we find rest. In Him, we find freedom. In Him is deliverance. We find it all in Him. Disappointment should not seep in if we do not receive everything by coming to Jesus. Grow in Him. In the process, you will be surprised what you will find.

As They Walked, They Got Healed

Jesus entered a village where 10 lepers asked Him to heal them. Instead of praying for them, touching them, or speaking a word of healing – Jesus told them to go and see the priest. "And so, it was that as they went, they were cleansed," (Luke 17:14). God healed them, not when they received prayer, but when they obeyed. Obedience to God can release His healing in our soul and body. Jesus heals when we pray and when we obey.

It is kind of like going to the doctor. Sometimes the doctor performs surgery on the spot and you leave completely whole. But for most of us, when we go to the doctor, he prescribes us medicine to take daily. As we follow his instructions, we see our health improve. Jesus is our doctor (see Mark 2:17) – He heals by His touch and by His word. If Jesus does not cure you when you pray, maybe it is time to take the prescription of His Word. "He sent His word and healed them and delivered them from their destructions," (Psalm 107:20). The Lord heals and delivers by His Word.

"My son, give attention to my words; incline your ear to my sayings. Do not let them depart from your eyes; keep them in the midst of your heart; for they are life to those who find them, and health to all their flesh," (Proverbs 4:20-22). The word "health" in this verse has an original meaning of health, healing, cure, and medicine. God's Word is like medicine. "The words that I speak to you are spirit, and they are life," (John 6:63). Healing and freedom may come when Jesus touches you, but at times, He gives you His Word so that you can walk in it. You will begin to see the Word change your situation.

Our Great Physician, Jesus, does not need a pharmacy. He has created His own medicine – one which carries absolutely no negative effects, no expiration date, and no bill at the end of the treatment. God's word is like medicine, a healing agent.

Medicine does not discriminate, so also is God's Word, when taken in it brings life.

God's word works as medicine, but only when you take it inside of you. Medicine does not work in the bottle and God's word does not work in the Bible. The Bible has to come inside of you. You have to take it in.

Medicine takes time to work, so does God's Word. You have to be patient as you walk in obedience with the Lord.

As you learn more about Jesus, you will find rest. As you walk in Jesus, you will get healed. There is power that is released in the process of growing in the Lord.

The River Grows Fuller as You Go Further

"And when the man went out to the east with the line in his hand, he measured 1,000 cubits, and he brought me through the waters; the water came up to my ankles," (Ezekiel 47:3). The Lord took prophet Ezekiel to the temple out of which water was flowing toward the east, toward the dead sea. After walking in that water for 1,000 cubits, around 1,700 feet, the water increased to the depth of an ankle which is pretty shallow. Just enough to splash one's feet, but not enough to be able to swim in. As the prophet kept walking, the water depth increased gradually until 1,700 feet later, the water was to the height of his knees. After another 1,000 cubits the water was at his waistline. After another 1,700 feet, he could not walk anymore, he could only swim. The river started to get deeper and wider as he went further.

This is the key to increasing in God's anointing – keep on walking in the river toward the Dead Sea. This revelation became a foundation for my understanding of how God wants to increase His anointing. Sometime ago, I left town during my fasting period to seek the face of the Lord. He revealed to Me there, through this word, that anointing is like that river. It begins with the ankles and increases with time. We have to be faithful in our river walk. Our desire to know Holy Spirit more will take us to another level. It is a process. As you go further in your walk with Holy Spirit, the river of God's anointing will grow fuller. Learn to develop a relationship with Holy Spirit and do not stop that relationship when you plateau. Keep on walking, things will change. God will measure a new level for you.

Being in the river was not the only thing that caused it to increase, the direction which it was heading also played a role. It was headed to the Dead Sea, the lowest point on earth. The Dead Sea represents people who are in their lowest point in life right now, in sin. Growing in God gets you closer to Holy Spirit and closer to people outside of the church. There is a purpose in bringing the Gospel to them. As we do that, He increases the depth and width of His river in our life until it comes to a time where that river brings healing and life to others.

Truly, during growth time, freedom, healing, and God's anointing increases in your life.

Prayer

"When I was weary and tired, I came to You, Jesus, and You gave me rest. Today, I ask You to give me Your yoke and burden. Teach me to be more like You. Teach me humility and meekness. Let me find rest, healing, freedom, and increase in my life as I live my life learning at Your feet."

CHAPTER 13

A TALE OF TWO SAULS

I come from a large extended family. My grandmother from my mother's side, who is still alive as I am writing this book, has 16 children, 73 grandchildren and 33 great grandchildren. My grandpa, her husband, already went to be with the Lord long ago. Some of my best memories are from my childhood. Growing up in a strong Ukrainian family that was strict Pentecostal had its blessings and burdens. I felt like the Scripture that was practiced more than any other was the verse about not sparing the rod from a child.

I remember my cousin and I were hanging out at my grandma's house. His dad, who was strict, told us not to leave grandma's house and wander off. We were around seven years of age. Of course, my cousin was more interested in adventure than obeying the strict rules of his dad, and I just wanted to follow my cousin, even though I warned him that his dad would not be happy if we got caught leaving the house.

We left grandma's house and wandered into some fields and more unknown places, and lost track of time. It turned out that we missed lunch, and everyone was looking for us. That was not a good thing. When we came back, we tried to join everyone as though we had done nothing wrong, but of course, that did not work. My uncle took both of us into the house and his son got a good, Ukrainian Pentecostal, spanking. It was a passionate one with a belt on his bare butt. I was watching this painful scene, holding my hands on my butt, knowing I would be next, because we both heard his father and both disobeyed him.

After his whipping was done and the Scripture was fulfilled, his dad looked at me in hot displeasure and said, "Get out from here." I thought, "That's it, no belt for me?" I ran from that house as quickly as I could, thanking God for causing that belt to skip over me and feeling bad for my cousin. Do you know why my uncle did not discipline me? Because I was not his son. In anger, he asked me to leave his house, but did not discipline me.

Fathers discipline their children. Fathers discipline, because children do not discipline themselves. If we were responsible, and stayed away from the neighbors' houses and fields, my cousin would never have gotten the spanking. Remember, as a Christian, you either discipline yourself or your loving Father will discipline you (see Hebrews 12:3-11, 1 Corinthians 11:32).

Be Like Any Other Man

God does not punish us for our sins — that already happened on the cross. God punished Jesus for all of our sin. As a loving Father, when we avoid living in discipline, He disciplines us to develop within us the fruit of holiness.

Discipline is different than punishment:

Punishment is eternal, discipline is temporary.

Punishment is for sinners, discipline is for saints.

Punishment is out of wrath, discipline is out of love.

Punishment is later, discipline is now.

Punishment casts a person out of God's presence, discipline draws them closer.

As it was with my cousin, his father disciplined him out of love, while keeping him in the house. I on the other hand, avoided getting spanked, but I got kicked out of the house. People in this world who break God's commandments will go to eternal separation from Him, even if it seems like their sins do not get them into trouble here on earth. As for us, God's children, when we refuse to walk in obedience to our Father, He will discipline us, here and now, to develop within us a new obedient character.

Samson thought that if his hair got cut off, there would be no problem. He would, "be like any other man," (Judges 16:7, 11, 17). Three times he told Delilah what needed to be done for him to be like any other man. Samson was deceived, he thought that by disobeying God, it would be to him like it was to everyone else.

People in the world who do not serve God, still live somehow, get married, have families and seem to even have fun. As much as Samson enjoyed the power and purpose he had, he did not think that living life without discipline would lead to anything except an ordinary, average life, similar to those around him.

When Samson did not discipline himself to stay away from alcohol, touch the dead, or cut his hair, he did not become like every other man. He got spanked. It was hard. The girl he loved left him for money. His eyes got gouged out. His freedom was lost. He spent the rest of his days going in circles. That is not how average men live, even the ungodly live better. You may say, well it is not worth it to be a Christian if God will discipline you for wrongdoing.

If you refuse to live a disciplined life as a believer, you will get disciplined by your Father. In the light of eternity, it is better to get a few spankings here on earth and stay close to the Father than to get cast out into outer darkness for eternity. There is only one way to avoid getting disciplined – it is to choose discipline. It is so much easier, more rewarding, and Holy Spirit will help us along the way if we choose the path of obedience. Yes, discipline is a narrow path, but it leads to life. A fulfilled, abundant, and victorious life. A life we dream of, and the life God has for us. It is a small price for us to pay for living in God's will. Remember, you will always pay a high price to live a life of sin and compromise.

Experience Must Lead to Discipline

There are two parallel stories that show how powerful a life of discipline is as it relates to following our encounter with God. I call it "A Tale of Two Sauls." One is a king, another is a Pharisee. One goes to Ramah to kill David, another goes to Damascus to kill Christians. Both think they are doing what is right. Both encounter God in a powerful and unusual way. King Saul prophesied naked all day and night. Saul from Tarsus was blind for three days.

The result of these two encounters is so different. King Saul becomes an apostate; Saul of Tarsus becomes an apostle. Both had incredible experiences, but one chose to go back to his old life. The other turned around completely and gave up his old life and embraced a new life which was the opposite of what it was before. One Saul died committing suicide, known as a murderer of priests; the other Saul died as a martyr, who chose to follow God's will until the end.

As powerful as your deliverance might have been, it has to be followed with a life fully dedicated to God, or else your powerful experience will do absolutely nothing in the long-term. I love awesome encounters with God, conference experiences, camp revivals, but all of that is given to us to spark a fire that will keep on burning. There is more. Your spiritual life is a walk, not a spiritual jump. We must learn to live in discipline, not just have leaps of crazy experiences that lead back to our old ways.

A few days ago, my wife and I rode our 49cc Yamaha moped around a farm area. We saw pigs playing in the mud. It was the same farm that I borrowed a pig from for a sermon illustration when I was a youth pastor. You can wash and clean a pig, but once you put it back into the farm, it will find its way to the mud and be back there again. That is how many of us see our encounters with God. We get washed and cleansed, only to run back and do the very things that offend the heart of God. What is the cure? Kill the pig on the cross and become a sheep by surrendering your will to God. Submit your flesh to the discipline of obedience to God. Discipline is important because it is the only way to defeat the flesh.

Satan, The World, and The Flesh

As I have mentioned before, we have been freed not to do what we want, but to do what we ought. A train can be freed from the train tracks and it can do what it wants to do, but it cannot get anywhere without being on those tracks. The two tracks that our freedom travels on are discipline and discipleship.

Deliverance gets the Devil out, but the life of discipline keeps him out. Deliverance is what God does for us, discipline is what He does in us.

Why is discipline so important? Because we have three enemies, which we face all the time and at times, the same time. Our enemies are the world (our outside enemy), the Devil (our invisible enemy), and the flesh (our inward enemy).

The Devil is overcome when fought by using God's Word in the power of Holy Spirit.

The world is overcome by fleeing like Joseph did from the scene of temptation. We flee from people and places that pull us down into our old paths.

The flesh is our worst enemy, because we cannot cast it out. Even after it is crucified by self-denial, it gets resurrected the next day. Feeding our spirit by fasting for the purpose of seeking God, helps us to overcome the flesh.

The Rod of Discipline

We all need discipline after we are freed from a particular bondage, but some people need discipline to be free. When addressing the issue of the cause of sin, Jesus did not suggest deliverance, but brutal discipline. "If your right eye causes you to sin, pluck it out and cast it from you; for it is more profitable for you that one of your members perish, than for your whole body to be cast into hell," (Matthew 5:29). Jesus, who is King of the spiritual world, knows the power of the Devil working behind the scenes of sin in the world. His advice to deal with different sins is putting your life through discipline, which is not pleasant. Being able to endure pain equivalent to cutting off your hand – that is brutal. Sometimes that kind of discipline is what brings breakthrough in your life.

If you do not discipline yourself, life will discipline you. It is better to discipline yourself than to get disciplined by life. To me, discipline involves regularly putting my flesh on the cross. As a believer I come to the cross for salvation, but I get up to die on the cross for my sanctification. Overcoming the flesh requires dying from your own ambition and sin through discipline and feeding the spirit.

Whatever you feed will grow; whatever you starve will die. "Walk in the Spirit, and you shall not fulfill the lust of the flesh," (Galatians 5:16). Flesh has lusts – lust is like having the medical condition athlete's foot. The more you scratch it, the more it itches. The flesh will never get satisfied; there is never enough. The only solution we have for our flesh is to put it on the cross. Walking in the Spirit helps to do that.

What Paul says, though, is that if we get closer to God, our flesh does not disappear, we simply get the power to stop catering to its demands. If you crucify your flesh, it gets resurrected the next day or week. It is important to prioritize walking with the Lord, which empowers you to avoid fulfilling the lust of the flesh. The lust of the flesh will not go away, but you will be able to stop fulfilling it. The itch will still be there, but you will have the power not to scratch it and eventfully the itch will go down.

Recently, I received insight from a well-known verse. A verse I have known since childhood, since my parents used it to discipline me. "Folly is bound up in the heart of a child, but the rod of discipline will drive it far away," (Proverbs 22:15, NIV). Sometimes, things get bound in our heart, perhaps not in our life, but our heart attaches to something that does have potential to draw us away from God. There is power that drives that away, it is called the rod of discipline. The rod indicates that putting discipline into your life is not like eating sweet candy. In fact, it might hurt for a while, but it will be worth it in the future.

During childhood, our parents applied that rod to us children. Now grown up, we have to learn to apply discipline in our own lives.

Discipleship Connects to Destiny

Discipleship is crucial to maintain your freedom and reach your destiny. A bound donkey was released by Jesus' followers and brought to Him. The same disciples that freed this donkey, now guided it until Jesus sat on it. Allowing people to walk beside us in our Christian walk is the key to not missing our destiny. Discipleship comes with a price. You have to humble yourself, commit to accountability, honor your parents, listen to your pastor, and attend a small group. When you are under the cover of your mentors and parents, it is like having an umbrella, which protects you from bad things in life.

We all learn either from mistakes or mentors. Mistakes teach us a lesson after we get hurt, mentors teach us a lesson to avoid getting hurt. Maybe someone will object that they do not need anyone but the Lord, Jesus Christ. Well, before Jesus sat on the donkey, that donkey was guided by His followers.

Before getting anointed for ministry, Jesus, Himself, lived in submission to His parents. In ministry, He was never doing what He pleased, instead He did what His Heavenly Father showed and desired of Him. He went from obeying earthly parents, to obeying, unto death, His Heavenly Father. No wonder Jesus had such authority when He spoke. He lived under authority.

You cannot walk in authority if you do not live under authority. Honor towards one's parents is where discipleship begins. Obedience is not the same as honor. Obedience is an action, honor is an attitude. We obey because it is the right thing to do, but we honor because there is a reward for it. Out of 10 commandments, the only commandment with an attached reward is honoring your father and mother. So many mistakes were avoided in my life because I obeyed my parents and pastor.

The purpose of our parents' existence in our lives, is to shape and direct us for our destiny. Joseph ended up in Egypt, where he prospered, but it started with him doing simple tasks his dad asked, such as bringing food to his brothers. Saul found his kingdom by running errands for his dad, not by trying to be a king. David fought Goliath, but he was on that field delivering food for the army, something his dad asked him to do. These men were not looking for their destiny, destiny found them. Instead they were busy doing whatever was presented to them by their parents. They were obeying their parents, not only praying and fasting to be used by God. There is a curse when dishonoring your parents. On the flip side, there is a huge blessing in living a life honoring one's parents.

Discipleship builds our character, it directs us toward our destiny and holds us accountable. Joshua needed Moses. David needed Samuel. Elisha needed Elijah. The disciples needed Jesus. Timothy needed Paul. We all need pastors, parents, and mentors, to help and direct us, to shape our character, and protect us from pride and foolishness.

Learn to honor your mentors, listen to your advisors, or you will be needing to learn from your mistakes.

Prayer

"After I have been exposed to sin, and am now encountering Your love Jesus, I know I cannot be the same again. I am ruined for good. I do not want to live average. I do not want to be like others. I want to follow You, Jesus. Give me the right mentors in my life, but most importantly, give me the right attitude toward those that You have already brought around me."

CHAPTER 14

RAISED TO DELIVER

At the age of 15, a young boy named Shavarsh got in a fight with a group of guys who beat him, tied a stone around his neck, threw him into a lake and left. He managed to remove the ropes around his hands, the stone around his neck, and swam to the surface of the lake. This experience led him to take swimming lessons. He quickly rose to the top in the sport of swimming by becoming a champion of Armenia at the age of 17. He went from being a "master of sports of the Soviet Union" to "master of international class" to "European champion" by breaking the world record. In the sport of swimming, he achieved incredible heights – 17 world championships in fin swimming, 13 European championships in fin swimming, and 7 Soviet championships in fin swimming.[12]

Apart from just his swimming championships, his life is also one of the most remarkable examples of how we are called to help others. One time, while riding a bus to his swimming school, the driver lost control behind the wheel on a dangerous mountain road and almost drove off the cliff. Shavarsh jumped into the driver's seat and helped to steer the bus onto the right path, saving 30 lives including his own.

Two years later, on September 16th, 1976, while running the usual 12 miles with his brother, he saw a trolleybus carrying 92 people, lose control and fly off the road into the freezing water. The bus fell into the Yerevan Lake. The trolleybus lay at the bottom of the lake about 80 feet away from the shore at a depth of 33 feet. Not wasting any time, Shavarsh Karapetyan ran to that reservoir and swam into it, despite the bad conditions. He broke the back window of the bus with both of his legs. He spent about 30 minutes in that frigid water and accomplished about 30 dives down to the wreck of the bus. His brother took care of the injured people as he went down to rescue them. One by one, he pulled out a lot of people, but only 20 of those he pulled out were alive and survived. (I actually met a lady in Florida who was 13 years of age during this event and lived near that lake. She was happy to hear the story of courage and salvation from her town all the way in USA.)

After his 30th dive, he fell unconscious. This act of courage ended his swimming career right there and almost cost him his life. Due to cold water and multiple lacerations from glass shards, he was left unconscious for 45 days. It took two years before the Russian paper published an article entitled, "The Underwater Battle of the Champion." He was given recognition and received a lot of support letters.

During an interview, they asked him what the most horrifying part of was, he responded:

"I knew that I could only save so many lives, I was afraid to make a mistake. It was so dark down there that I could barely see anything. On one of my dives, I accidentally grabbed a seat instead of a passenger... I could have saved a life instead. That seat still haunts me in my nightmares."[13]

I am so inspired by this modern-day hero who leveraged his life to save others around him. At times it endangered his own health. His only regret was that he did not help more people. Heroes come in all shapes and sizes, but one thing they have in common is they are willing to put their life on the line to save others. I am not impressed with actors, artists, athletes – real heroes are those who reflect God's nature. They live for what Jesus died for – souls. If you make it your goal to save people, God will turn you from zero to hero. Your trial will become your testimony, and your mess will turn into a message.

You are Loosed to be Used

"Go into the village opposite you, and immediately you will find a donkey tied, and a colt with her. Loose them and bring them to Me," (Matthew 21:2). The real purpose behind freeing the donkey was to provide a vehicle for Jesus to ride into Jerusalem. Jesus needed a ride to the city. His Uber was the donkey. Still, today, Jesus wants to enter into the seven mountains of societal influence. He desires to enter into the church, the family, the education system, government, media, the arts & entertainment, and business. He desires to use us as vehicles that will carry His message and glory to these arenas.

You are loosed from robes of sin, addiction, and bondage so that you can be used by the Lord for His purpose. After salvation and freedom, make it your life's aim to live for Him and His will. Do not reduce the purpose of your life to only getting married, starting a family, building a home, going on vacations, paying off your home, and saving for retirement. There is nothing wrong with getting your life established, but for a Christian who has been rescued by Jesus' death, whose home is in Heaven, who knows that hell is hot and eternity is long – to live for anything less than what Jesus died for is wrong!

At times, we think that in order to live out God's will we have to quit our job and move out as missionaries. Some people are called to do that, but for the rest of us, Jesus sets us free so that He can send us to our places of influence as missionaries. A missionary is more of a mindset than a location. It is living with intention to bring the Kingdom into the place of your influence. Our job is to go into the world carrying Jesus. Holy Spirit begins to create opportunities for miracles to happen around those we are called to impact.

As Jesus sat on the donkey, it became transportation for Him into the city. When Holy Spirit comes upon us, He sits on us, to empower us to be His witnesses. Holy Spirit is in me for my sake, but He is upon me for the sake of others.

Baptism of the Holy Spirit is not limited to tongues and prayer life, instead, the Spirit comes to sit on you to make you a donkey that will carry Jesus into your Jerusalem. Sadly, we Pentecostals have reduced the baptism of the Spirit to speaking in tongues. It is more than that. You will receive power to be witnesses – that is the real goal for baptism. I know many who speak in tongues, but never bring people to church. They do not share their faith, nor do they care about the work of missions. It does not bother them that the church they attend has not seen people getting saved for years. No wonder, since the only thing they received was tongues, not power.

The purpose for freedom and getting filled with the Spirit is for us to be witnesses. We are not empowered by the Spirit to be lawyers who debate, but witnesses who share what we have seen and heard. God does not anoint us to win debates, but to win souls. This is the ultimate goal for freedom.

Born for Such a Time as This

"For if you remain completely silent at this time, relief and deliverance will arise for the Jews from another place, but you and your father's house will perish. Yet who knows whether you have come to the kingdom for such a time as this?" (Esther 4:14). Esther is a heroine from the Bible who leveraged her platform for the fulfillment of God's purpose. Things did not start well for her. She was named Hadassah by her parents, whom she lost when Israel got invaded by Babylon. An orphan became a captive. Her relative Mordecai adopted her and changed her name to Esther.

King Xerxes' wife dishonored him, thus forfeiting her crown. The place of queen became vacant. Agents were seeking good looking girls to fill her place and Esther was one of the women who were chosen. Favor on her life put her on the top and she was chosen to be the wife of the king. She was blessed; some would call her very lucky. From zero to hero, from rags to riches. But God had a different plan for her platform. Her new position had a purpose. That purpose became evident when her people were under the threat of annihilation. Her life was comfortable at the palace. Mordecai lived in both worlds, in the palace and outside of it. He saw the anguish and death facing his people, something Esther was out of touch with. He brought conviction to her that her palace had a purpose.

Holy Spirit is our Mordecai, who is aware of the future facing our world, for those who do not know Jesus. He knows that those who do not receive Jesus face eternal emotional anguish, physical torment, spiritual separation, and many are headed into a Christ-less eternity.

The Spirit seeks to disturb our comfort with conviction. As Mordecai told Esther, so the Spirit is telling us, that we were raised up for a reason. God saved you, to save others. God raised you, to lift others. It is not because you were better than others that you obtained mercy and favor. Had it not been for the love of God, you would be no different than the masses who are headed to hell without salvation. You may wonder why God is not doing something about it. Actually, He did everything! The question is — why are you not doing something about it? Have we done anything for that purpose? Have we done everything?

The Spirit of God is there to remind us to be willing to pay a price to make the purpose of saving people as our highest priority.

Many people love to save others, as long as it is convenient, costing them nothing. That is the problem! Anytime you are dealing with salvation, you must be willing to a pay a price. Risk your comfort, selfishness, and challenge your fears. Do not buy into the fear that you will lose your influence if you leverage it for the sake of salvation. That was Esther's fear. If she went to the King to beg for her nation, she would die. Esther did not lose her crown by laying it down to save her nation. Most of us will not lose when we seek to save others. But even if we experience temporary loss of our comfort for the sake of our calling – it is a small price to pay compared with the eternal dividends.

It is sad to see influential, rich people in high places of society, afraid to let their light shine out of political correctness or fear to offend. They reduce their calling of bringing salvation to merely providing inspiration. It is becoming a trend to be inspirational. There is nothing wrong with that idea, but it cannot be a goal for those who know that hell is hot and forever is too long. I can only imagine what would happen if Esther would say, "Mordecai, this whole salvation thing is a bit risky and I could lose my position. I will live my life as queen to inspire little girls all around Babylon to dream big dreams."

When you know people are going to die, living to inspire others is missing the point. We are called to bring salvation, not merely to provide inspiration to a dying generation. If a man is walking to a cliff, he does not need inspiration, he needs you to guide him away from it. If a house is burning, the people in it do not need inspiration, but to be rescued. If a person is drowning, he does not need encouragement to "hang in there," he needs a savior. Jesus did not come to inspire, but to save those who are lost.

Delivered to Deliver

Before Moses was born, it says "...the children of Israel groaned because of the bondage, and they cried out; and their cry came up to God because of their bondage. God heard their groaning, and God remembered His covenant with Abraham, with Isaac, and with Jacob," (Exodus 2:23-24). Moses' birth was an answer to the cry of people in bondage. God protected him from being killed in the river. He was spared from death on purpose, not because he was lucky, or better than others. Maybe you have been spared from so many things that people in our generation are struggling with. It is not because you were born into a better family, or you made better choices. There was a hand of God on your life. It is there on purpose, not to exalt or show how great you are, but so you would become a tool in God's hand for salvation.

Moses was exposed to the palace like Esther. The palace can make you comfortable and a bit prideful, thinking you are there because you worked hard. If you think, "I deserve this," then you have missed the whole point of your existence.

Shortly after, Moses got exposed to the pain of others by visiting his brothers and sisters who were slaves. Exposure to the pain of others produces new perspective. You cannot live in the palace the same way any longer. When you see poverty in a third world country, or visit homeless shelters, minister in jail, or visit those on their death bed, your perspective changes. If you want to obtain compassion for the lost, put your heart in the place where people's pain is at. Do not be a Pharisee who saw a bleeding man on the road and crossed over to the other side to avoid getting close to the suffering of humanity. This exposure messed Moses up. He became angry, took the matter into his own hands and tried to bring justice. Moses was not indifferent to the bondage of others. That is what God liked about him. He made mistakes, but being indifferent was not one of them.

Moses' outburst of anger ended the life of an Egyptian and it cost him 40 years in the wilderness. Then God came. Moses obtained exposure to the presence of God, which gave him purpose. Before he found his purpose, he killed people. In God's presence, he went on to save people. God's presence will always lead you to your purpose. Your purpose will be to help others. Have you been exposed to the palace which resulted in comfort? Have you experienced exposure to the pain of the broken world, and has it resulted in a change of your perspective? You still need to be exposed to God's presence for God's purpose to be activated in your life.

God sent Moses to a place where he used to be, where people were just like him. God wants to send you to your generation to bring salvation, healing, and deliverance. The reason why you are where you are now is because of God's mercy and for His purpose. God raised you up for a reason. Accept the reason as His will, which is that none shall perish, but that all will come to know Jesus as their Savior.

Called to Answer the Cry

"Now therefore, behold, the cry of the children of Israel has come to Me, and I have also seen the oppression with which the Egyptians oppress them. Come now, therefore, and I will send you to Pharaoh that you may bring My people, the children of Israel, out of Egypt," (Exodus 3:9-10). God prepared Moses for His calling by the things He took him through. Being in the palace, he knew how to address those in the palace. Being in the wilderness, he knew how to lead a nation through the wilderness. Being in God's presence, he knew how to lead people to meet God. Everything you are going through is to prepare you for your purpose.

The call of God on Moses was an answer to the cry of the oppressed people in Egypt. God would not be calling if people would not be crying. I pray to the Lord that you understand this in your spirit. The only reason why God calls you is because He is answering the cry of your generation. God cannot answer the cry unless you answer the call. God wanted to make it clear to Moses that He was not calling him to this powerful ministry to make him famous and powerful, but to answer the groaning of the hurting people.

This became real to me, years ago, when I moved into my house close to the church. I had met my neighbors and was planning to invite one of them to church a bit later, after I settled down. The church is a few blocks from my house. I kept pushing it off to another, more opportune, time. After a while, I stopped seeing my neighbor. One day while I was rollerblading with my wife, she mentioned to me that she had a heavy feeling about our neighbor. I told her I had not seen him for months. A few days after this, I saw FBI vehicles turning the whole place upside down. I decided to go online and searched his social media profile and Googled his name. It turned out that my neighbor had been dead for the past two months already. Man, was I convicted. I kept postponing sharing my faith, and now he was dead.

A few months later, the house got put up for sale and the real estate agent came to me as I was washing my car in my driveway. She asked if I wanted to go and see the house. I declined saying that I was not interested in buying another house. She said, "Oh no, not to buy, just to see." I decided to go and see the house so she would leave me alone.

I toured the house with her and noticed in the living room that there was an 8-feet by 4-feet piece of carpet missing right in the middle of the living room. I made a remark that it is strange to have carpet everywhere besides in the middle of the living room. She responded, "You don't know how he died?" I said, "No, I don't. How did he die?" Her answer hit me like a ton of bricks and it made sense why God had been putting him on my heart. The agent said, "He committed suicide in the living room." I could barely hold back my tears. I left that house and ran home, closed myself in my room and, wept for a while. I cried, I repented, and promised not to ignore God's promptings again.

There, in my room, God reminded me of the verse, when He called Moses to help Israel. It was to answer the cry of the people. He told me that when He called me to help that man, He was trying to answer the cry of his heart, but I never responded. I got it. My calling was to answer someone's cry. I cannot ignore my calling anymore. I have to be eager to fulfill it. There will be people who will get saved and delivered, because you and I answer the call. There will be individuals, families, and even cities changed when we answer the call.

Jonah ran from the call of God. The Bible says that he ran from God's presence. When you run from God's purpose, you run from God, period. Little did Jonah know that answering the call would allow God to answer the cry of the whole city and save it.

Answer the call. Let God answer their cry. You are free from Egypt, to free others from Egypt. Do not buy into excuses that you are too young, too old, too inexperienced, cannot speak, do not have money, or don't have connections – get a burning fire in your heart for the lost, and Holy Spirit will bring the rest.

Prayer

"Jesus, You said that You will make those who follow You fishers of men. Mold me into a person who will live with eternity in mind. I pray that You will anoint me to make an impact on my generation and help me to live with intention. Give me greater compassion for the lost and the

dying. Use me to rescue people from eternal death. Holy Spirit, give me opportunities today to share my faith."

APPENDIX 1

HOW TO GET SAVED?

"Believe on the Lord Jesus Christ, and you will be saved," (Acts 16:31).

Before you can believe in Jesus as your Savior, you need to know what you need to be saved from. An umbrella saves you from getting wet. A helmet saves you from getting hurt. Jesus can save you from the punishment and power of your sin.

Each one of us have sinned against God (see Romans 3:23). Even if we try to be really good, we still fall short of God's perfect standard. We sin against God every day by not obeying His commands in the Bible, such as loving Him best, honoring our parents, and telling the truth.

God is holy (perfect and separate from sin), He will punish unbelieving sinners by separating them to a place of eternal death: hell (see Romans 6:23). Due to God's great love, He sent His own Son to save believers from this punishment by dying on the Cross in their place. Then Jesus rose from the dead, proving His victory over sin and death.

"If you confess with your mouth the Lord Jesus and believe in your heart that God has raised Him from the dead, you will be saved. For with the heart one believes unto righteousness, and with the mouth confession is made unto salvation," (Romans 10:9-10).

If you would like to receive Jesus Christ and His salvation, please pray this prayer:

"I come to You, Jesus, to give You my heart and my life. I confess You as the Lord of my life, instead of myself. I ask You to forgive me of my

sins and make me clean. I ask this, because I believe You paid the price for every wrongdoing and sin I've ever committed. I, now, receive into my heart Your righteousness and declare that I am saved, and Your child!"

Welcome to the family of God and your new life in Christ!

STUDY GUIDE

Introduction - Lion Killer

Key Scripture: 1 Samuel 17:34-37

Points to Ponder:

- Before you can fight Goliath publicly, you must face lions privately.
- Deliverance is a process which involves identifying, confronting and resisting the enemy.

Food for Thought:

1. What prompted you to pick up this book?
2. Did some areas of your life encourage you to select a book on freedom?
3. On a scale of 1 to 10, with 1 being "totally in bondage" and 10 being "living in full victory," how much would you rate your current stance concerning freedom? Why did you choose that number?
4. In which areas of your life are you currently facing lions and bears?
5. Have you experienced any demonic activity when you prayed or ministered to others?
6. True or False. Every person who wants to be used by God, first must get possessed by the devil, so that they can relate better to oppressed people.

Chapter 1 - Don't Beat the Donkey

Key Scripture: Ephesians 6:10-20

Points to Ponder:

- Satan is behind sin.
- A natural war removes evil people, a spiritual war removes evil out of people.
- God anointed you to win battles with the Devil, not arguments with people.

Food for Thought:

1. Why do you think Jesus performed deliverances publicly?
2. Do you have areas of your life currently, where you are dealing with symptoms instead of the root of the issue?
3. Do you know someone who was a really evil person, but after God set them free, they are the nicest person? Share their story!
4. Why do you think there was less casting out of demons in the Old Testament?
5. True or False. Jesus viewed the ministry of deliverance as a private practice hidden from the public eye.

Chapter 2 – Six Demon Spirits

Key Scripture: Mark 5:1-20

Points to Ponder:

- Demons are unclean spirits that love to live in unclean places.
- Evil spirits seek to occupy people, animals, and territories.
- All evil spirits have the same goal to entice, harass, torment, enslave, defile, deceive, and attack the body.
- Names of evil spirits mentioned include: spirit of fear, spirit of python, spirit of lust, spirit of pride, spirit of infirmity and spirit of bondage.

- Insects bite to suck blood, snakes bite to release poison, but pythons kill by squeezing its victim.

Food for Thought:

1. Which evil principality is influencing and ruling your region? Do you pray against it?
2. Why do you think Jesus let the demons speak, since their master is the father of lies?
3. What are some functions of the spirit of fear? Spirit of lust? Spirit of addiction? Spirit of python? Spirit of infirmity? Spirit of pride?
4. How different is the python from all other snakes? How does it relate to spiritual warfare?
5. Out of six spirits mentioned in the Bible, which do you see having influence in your family and your personal life?
6. True or False. We can ask demons about anything that interests us.

Chapter 3 - Open Doors

Key Scripture: Ephesians 4:27-30

Points to Ponder:

- The Devil is a thief who operates at night and in secrecy.
- The Devil is like a dog on a leash, he can only bark at Christians but cannot bite them if they stay away from his territory.
- Getting into the occult is an open door for demons.
- Accursed things bring a curse into your life.
- Rejection breeds rebellion.

Food for Thought:

1. How is the nature of our enemy consistent with the profile of a thief?

2. Have you ever been involved in the occult? Why?
3. After reading the part about accursed things, does anything come to your mind, that you might possess, that should be removed or prayed against?
4. What are some of the ways that people can get demons through trauma?
5. True or False. If you have been abused, you can be 100% sure that you have demons.

Chapter 4 - Grave Clothes

Key Scripture: Deuteronomy 28

Points to Ponder:

- Whatever is blessed multiplies; whatever is cursed withers.
- Signs of curses are premature death, breakdown of families, accident proneness, repeated negative destiny of parents, chronic sicknesses, fears and phobias, constant poverty.
- There are three types of curses: generational curses, cast curses, and earned curses.

Food for Thought:

1. What character and physical traits got passed down to you from your parents?
2. What negative things are you fighting right now, that have been in your family tree for as long as you can remember?
3. Have you had people in authority repeatedly speak negative things into your life?
4. Which phrase or statement have you said about yourself regularly, that does not line up with the Word of God?
5. What are the six open doors for curses?
6. Which one of those six sins brings a curse which you still have not repented of today in your life?

7. True or False. When you steal, you open the door to demons.

Chapter 5 – The Children's Bread

Key Scripture: Matthew 15:21-28

Points to Ponder:

- We are saved, we are being saved, and we shall be saved.
- Salvation is for the spirit, soul, and body.
- What bread is to the children, deliverance is to believers. Freedom is food.
- We do not fight for victory, we fight from victory.

Food for Thought:

1. Salvation is not an event, it is a process. What are the three stages of that process?
2. If Holy Spirit lives in the spirit of the Christian, where are the demons tormenting him when he is demonized?
3. What does the Greek word "Sozo" mean?
4. What are the 10 things Jesus provided by His death on Calvary?
5. What five animals does the Scripture compare the Devil to? How do they reveal the Devil's task?
6. True or False. The Devil is defeated; therefore, he is not a problem anymore.

Chapter 6 - Find Freedom

Key Scripture: John 8:31-36

Points to Ponder:

- Bondage is deceptive, most people who are in bondage are convinced that they are free.

- Confessing sin opens the door for deliverance. Repentance from sin closes the door to demons.
- If you want to walk in authority, you must live under authority of the Lordship of Jesus Christ.
- The process of deliverance involves recognizing the enemy, repenting from sin, rebuking the enemy, resisting the enemy, replacing the enemy with God, and renewing our mind. They all begin with the prefix "re."

Food for Thought:

1. Have you ever met someone who was bound by an addiction or demon, yet they were certain that they were not in bondage? Why is that?
2. What does it mean to repent? Give an example from your life.
3. Are you in a place, right now, where you just keep giving Jesus "more room" instead of giving Him "the key" to the whole house of your life?
4. If the Devil comes back after your deliverance with his army of doubt, fear, and temptation, what will you do?
5. True or False. When you confess the sins of your forefathers, it gives them a second chance with God if they went to hell.

Chapter 7 – The Bait of Satan

Key Scripture: Matthew 18:21-35

Points to Ponder:

- There can be no freedom without forgiveness.
- An offense is the bait for the Devil.
- Wounds neglected become infected. Wounds say you have been hurt, scars testify that you have been healed.
- You must forgive others, yourself, and God.

Food for Thought:

1. What does the Greek word "Skandalon" mean? How does it relate to the Devil's plan to destroy us?
2. What is the difference between wounds and scars?
3. What is the difference between betrayal and bitterness?
4. Why is holding onto unforgiveness so damaging?
5. Who is the hardest person to forgive?
6. What does it mean to "forgive God?"
7. True or False. You should forgive yourself because if you do not, you are telling God that you are holier than Him.

Chapter 8 - Motive for Freedom

Key Scripture: 2 Corinthians 3:17

Points to Ponder:

- Freedom is not doing what you want, it is doing what you ought.
- God sets us free so that we serve Him, not so we can be more selfish.

Food for Thought:

1. What was your real reason for seeking freedom? Be honest with yourself.
2. What was the reason God told Pharaoh to take Israel out of captivity?
3. What is the difference between the attitude "give me" and "make me," as portrayed in the story of the prodigal son? What way do you lean towards in your attitude?
4. True or False. When someone is no longer addicted, that is when they are truly free.

Chapter 9 - Breaking Strongholds

Key Scripture: 2 Corinthians 10:4

Points to Ponder:

- The strongman is a demon, a stronghold is a house of thoughts. The strongman comes quickly and usually exits quickly. Strongholds that are built over time get destroyed over time.
- You can control your mind, but your mindset controls you.
- Truth is like soap, it only works when it is applied.
- Our mind is like a ship – once it gets hit by the icebergs of life, it gets holes and the surrounding water starts to slip inside, creating a stronghold.
- Christians can have three mentalities: a slave, a survivor, and a soldier.

Food for Thought:

1. What is the difference between demonic possession and a stronghold?
2. What are the two main ways Jesus offered freedom to come in, from in the book of John, chapter 8?
3. When things were not going well for Moses — Pharaoh was not budging, the Israelites were upset, and Moses was frustrated — what did God offer as a solution to Moses?
4. Which one of the three mindsets currently occupy your thinking?
5. What should you do if you only get partial victory?
6. True or False. God created man for the purpose of being delivered.

Chapter 10 - Renewing of the Mind

Key Scripture: Romans 12:2

Points to Ponder:

- Where the mind goes, man follows.

- God wants to bring a miracle in your mind before He fixes the mess in your life.
- Faith is not hoping, it is having. It is a title deed for your miracle.

Food for Thought:

1. What did God create on Day One? How could light come without the sun?
2. What is faith?
3. What are the seven practical steps described to renew your mind? Which steps have you taken already? Which steps are you currently struggling with?
4. True or False. Renewal of the mind is like salvation, it all depends on God.

Chapter 11 - Stay on Fire

Key Scripture: Luke 12:35

Points to Ponder:

- Before we do something wrong, we usually do multiple things which are not wise. The reason why we excuse the unwise things is because they are usually not wrong.
- Flirting with sin typically leads to falling into sin.
- Grace is not an excuse to flirt with sin, it is the power to overcome sin.
- We are called to run to God, from sin, and with those who are of the same convictions.

Food for Thought:

1. What are practical ways you stay away from the ditch when you drive? How is that principle applicable to life's choices?
2. Why is it important to stay on fire for God?
3. What three things must we do to stay on fire for God?

4. True or False. You can throw your snakes into your pastor's fire.

Chapter 12 - As You Grow

Key Scripture: Matthew 11:28-29

Points to Ponder:

- There is freedom that comes when you come to Jesus, but there is also freedom that comes when you grow in Jesus.
- Do not let your issue become your identity.
- The river grows fuller as you go further.

Food for Thought:

1. How does a palm tree symbolize the Christian life?
2. What are two ways to get free from anxiety?
3. How is God's Word like medicine?
4. What are two things we must do to increase God's river in our life?
5. True or False. If you did not get free when someone prayed for you, your only other option is to look for someone else more powerful to pray for you.

Chapter 13 - Tale of Two Saul's

Key Scripture: Matthew 5:29

Points to Ponder:

- Punishment is for sinners, discipline is for saints.
- Every experience with God must lead to repentance toward God.
- We overcome the world by fleeing the flesh, by feeding the spirit, and by fighting the Devil with God's Word.

Food for Thought:

1. What are five differences between punishment and discipline?
2. If both Sauls had amazing encounters with God, why did each of them have a different ending?
3. Have you had an amazing encounter with God before? Did it change anything?
4. What are our three enemies and how do we overcome them?
5. What disciplines are currently lacking in your life that are hindering your destiny?
6. Who is currently discipling you toward fulfilling your calling?
7. True or False. You cannot discipline a demon and cast out the flesh.

Chapter 14 - Raised to Deliver

Key Scripture: Esther 4:14

Points to Ponder:

*   You are loosed so that you can be used.
*   Leverage your platform for salvation, not just mere inspiration.
*   Your calling is an answer to the cry.

Food for Thought:

1. From the story about the donkey, what do you think is the real purpose for our freedom?
2. What is your calling? Are you living toward it?
3. True or False. The calling of every Christian is to inspire others.

ABOUT THE AUTHOR

Vladimir Savchuk leads the HungryGen movement and pastors a multi-cultural church with a clear-cut, focused vision to see salvation of souls, healing, deliverance, and the raising up of young leaders. He leads the annual "Raised to Deliver" conferences, which attract thousands from all over the globe. He also leads two different internships, one for teens and another for young adults. Pastor Vlad is a sought-after speaker at conferences and camps.

Vlad was born in Ukraine and raised in a Christian home. He immigrated to the U.S. at the age of 13 and became a youth pastor at the age of 16. Recently, he became the lead pastor of the HungryGen Church.

He is married to his beautiful wife, Lana, with whom he enjoys spending time and doing ministry together.

STAY CONNECTED

Facebook.com/vladhungrygen

Twitter.com/vladhungrygen

Instagram.com/vladhungrygen

YouTube.com/vladimirsavchuk

If you have a testimony from reading this book, please email vlad@hungrygen.com

If you wish to post about this book on your social media, please use #pastorvlad #hungrygen #breakfreebook hashtags.

If you need a video study guide for a small group to go along with this book, you may find it at www.hungrygen.com

NOTES

[1] Bright, B. (2018, February 18). The World's Peace – Feb. 19. Retrieved from
https://www.christianity.com/devotionals/insights-from-bill-bright/the-world-s-peace-feb-19.html

[2] Occult. (n.d.). Retrieved June 10, 2018, from
http://www.dictionary.com/browse/occult?s=t

[3] Russian Phantom Death Care. (n.d.). Retrieved June 10, 2018, from
http://www.hauntedvehicles.com/jamesdeanspyder.html

[4] Dunlop, Aaron. (2014, October 28). The Juke – Edwards Story: A Constant in Family
https://thinkgospel.wordpress.com/2014/10/28/the-juke-edwards-story-a-contrast-in-family-legacy/

[5] The Mysteries of Chappaquiddick. (1969, August 1). Retrieved June 8, 2018, from
http://content.time.com/time/magazine/article/0,9171,901159-1,00.html

[6] Timeline: The Kennedy Curse. (2012, May 17). Retrieved June 8, 2018, from
https://www.telegraph.co.uk/news/worldnews/northamerica/usa/9271425/Timeline-the-Kennedy-Curse.html

[7] Proverbs 26. (n.d.). Retrieved June 10, 2018, from 1. https://www.biblestudytools.com/commentaries/matthew-henry-complete/proverbs/26.html

[8] Eckman, J. (2016, October 22). The Curse of Anti-Semitism. Retrieved June 8, 2018, from https://graceuniversity.edu/iip/2016/10/the-curse-of-anti-semitism/

[9] Suchard, J., & LoVecchio, F. (1999, June 17). Envenomations by Rattlesnakes Thought to Be Dead. Retrieved June 10, 2018, from https://www.nejm.org/doi/full/10.1056/NEJM199906173402420

[10] Chosen to Die, Destined to Live. (n.d.). Retrieved June 11, 2018, from https://candlesholocaustmuseum.org/file_download/inline/200 73489-b76a-4f74-a7ff-630efb9b1b1a

[11] Ten Egyptian Plagues For Ten Egyptian Gods and Goddesses. (n.d.). Retrieved June 14, 2018, from http://www.stat.rice.edu/~dobelman/Dinotech/10_Eqyptian_go ds_10_Plagues.pdf

[12] True Story of a Real life Superhero: Shavarsh Karapetyan. (2014, February 8). Retrieved June 16, 2018, from https://www.peopleofar.com/2014/02/08/true-story-of-a-real-life-superhero-shavarsh-karapetyan/

[13] Shavarsh Karapetyan - A Real Life Hero. (2014, February 4). Retrieved June 16, 2018, from https://kindnessblog.com/2014/02/04/shavarsh-karapetyan-a-real-life-hero/

Printed in the USA
CPSIA information can be obtained
at www.ICGtesting.com
LVHW010719031023
759897LV00020B/83/J

Made in the USA
Coppell, TX
01 March 2021